TEEN RIGHTS AND FREEDOMS

| Emancipation

TEEN RIGHTS AND FREEDOMS

I Emancipation

Noël Merino
Book Editor

GREENHAVEN PRESS
A part of Gale, Cengage Learning

GALE
CENGAGE Learning·

Farmington Hills, Mich • San Francisco • New York • Waterville, Maine
Meriden, Conn • Mason, Ohio • Chicago

Elizabeth Des Chenes, *Director, Content Strategy*
Douglas Dentino, *Manager, New Product*

For more information, contact:
Greenhaven Press
27500 Drake Rd.
Farmington Hills, MI 48331-3535
Or you can visit our Internet site at gale.cengage.com.

For product information and technology assistance, contact us at:

Gale Customer Support, 1-800-877-4253.
For permission to use material from this text or product, submit all requests online at www.cengage.com/permissions.

Further permissions questions can be emailed to permissionrequest@cengage.com.

Articles in Greenhaven Press anthologies are often edited for length to meet page requirements. In addition, original titles of these works are changed to clearly present the main thesis and to explicitly indicate the author's opinion. Every effort is made to ensure the Greenhaven Press accurately reflects the original intent of the authors. Every effort has been made to trace the owners of copyrighted material.

Cover Image © Eugenio Marongiu/Shutterstock.com.

LIBRARY OF CONGRESS CATALOGING-IN-PUBLICATION DATA

Emancipation / Noël Merino, book editor.
pages cm -- (Teen rights and freedoms)
Includes bibliographical references and index.
ISBN 978-0-7377-6999-9 (hardback)
1. Minors--United States--Juvenile literature. 2. Teenagers--Legal status, laws, etc.--United States--Juvenile literature. I. Merino, Noël, editor of compilation.
KF479.T44 2014
342.7308'772--dc23
2014011946

Printed in the United States of America
1 2 3 4 5 6 7 18 17 16 15 14

Contents

A reporter contends that emancipation is rare and usually only viable for rich child stars, with the general trend toward longer parental support.

despite the fact that emancipation is usually achieved at eighteen.

Foreword

*"In the truest sense freedom cannot be
  bestowed, it must be achieved."*
                                Franklin D. Roosevelt,
                                September 16, 1936

The notion of children and teens having rights is a relatively recent development. Early in American history, the head of the household—nearly always the father—exercised complete control over the children in the family. Children were legally considered to be the property of their parents. Over time, this view changed, as society began to acknowledge that children have rights independent of their parents, and that the law should protect young people from exploitation. By the early twentieth century, more and more social reformers focused on the welfare of children, and over the ensuing decades advocates worked to protect them from harm in the workplace, to secure public education for all, and to guarantee fair treatment for youths in the criminal justice system. Throughout the twentieth century, rights for children and teens—and restrictions on those rights—were established by Congress and reinforced by the courts. Today's courts are still defining and clarifying the rights and freedoms of young people, sometimes expanding those rights and sometimes limiting them. Some teen rights are outside the scope of public law and remain in the realm of the family, while still others are determined by school policies.

Each volume in the Teen Rights and Freedoms series focuses on a different right or freedom and offers an anthology of key essays and articles on that right or freedom and the responsibilities that come with it. Material within each volume is drawn from a diverse selection of primary and secondary sources— journals, magazines, newspapers, nonfiction books, organization newsletters, position papers, speeches, and government documents, with a particular emphasis on Supreme Court and lower court decisions. Volumes also include first-person narratives from young people and others involved in teen rights issues, such as parents and educators. The material is selected and arranged to highlight all the major social and legal controversies relating to the right or freedom under discussion. Each selection is preceded by an introduction that provides context and background. In many cases, the essays point to the difference between adult and teen rights, and why this difference exists.

Many of the volumes cover rights guaranteed under the Bill of Rights and how these rights are interpreted and protected in regard to children and teens, including freedom of speech, freedom of the press, due process, and religious rights. The scope of the series also encompasses rights or freedoms, whether real or perceived, relating to the school environment, such as electronic devices, dress, Internet policies, and privacy. Some volumes focus on the home environment, including topics such as parental control and sexuality.

Numerous features are included in each volume of Teen Rights and Freedoms:

- An annotated **table of contents** provides a brief summary of each essay in the volume and highlights court decisions and personal narratives.
- An **introduction** specific to the volume topic gives context for the right or freedom and its impact on daily life.
- A brief **chronology** offers important dates associated with the right or freedom, including landmark court cases.
- **Primary sources**—including personal narratives and court decisions—are among the varied selections in the anthology.
- **Illustrations**—including photographs, charts, graphs, tables, statistics, and maps—are closely tied to the text and chosen to help readers understand key points or concepts.

- An annotated list of **organizations to contact** presents sources of additional information on the topic.
- A **for further reading** section offers a bibliography of books, periodical articles, and Internet sources for further research.
- A comprehensive subject **index** provides access to key people, places, events, and subjects cited in the text.

Each volume of Teen Rights and Freedoms delves deeply into the issues most relevant to the lives of teens: their own rights, freedoms, and responsibilities. With the help of this series, students and other readers can explore from many angles the evolution and current expression of rights both historic and contemporary.

Introduction

Prior to becoming emancipated, children are considered minors under the law and lack many of the rights afforded adults. Minors' parents have rights over them until emancipation: For many legal matters, minors are dependent on their parents' consent or involvement. When minors reach the state-mandated age of majority, they are then treated as adults under the law. There are exceptions, however, both prior to the age of majority and after. For example, prior to the age of majority, minors may be considered emancipated for the purposes of certain health care decisions. And after the age of majority, minors do not gain all the rights of adults, such as the right to drink alcohol.

Laws concerning the emancipation of minors—the time at which parental rights are terminated—are set by state law. Each state sets its own laws regarding the age of majority, as does the District of Columbia. At the start of 2014, all states except for three set the age of majority at eighteen years of age. Alabama and Nebraska set the age of majority at nineteen years and Mississippi has set its age of majority at twenty-one years of age. Other situations in addition to age that can trigger emancipation are marriage (although the right to marry has age restrictions set by the states) and enlistment in military service (although the United States does not allow enlistment prior to the age of seventeen years).

States also set laws regarding procedures by which a minor can petition the courts for emancipation prior to the age of majority. In most cases, a parent or someone acting in the place of a parent must petition the court for emancipation, since a minor lacks the ability to petition the court. Emancipation prior to the age of majority is not given easily, and the minor must prove that emancipation is in his or her best interest. The minor usually must prove the ability to provide for herself or himself and in general, emancipation will not be granted against a competent parent's wishes. Whether or not emancipation is available prior to the age of majority, the earliest age at which a minor may petition for emancipation and the necessary criteria for the granting of emancipation vary widely from state to state.

Prior to emancipation a minor is under the care of his or her parent(s) or guardian, but the US Supreme Court and different state courts have determined that in certain situations a minor may be granted the ability to make some decisions without the involvement of a parent. Most of these cases have pertained to health care. The Supreme Court set a precedent in 1976 by striking down a state law that required parental consent—without any exceptions—in order for a minor to obtain an abortion. This case, *Planned Parenthood of Central Missouri v. Danforth*, was decided by the court just a few years after it established a woman's right to abortion in *Roe v. Wade* (1973). The Court also extended the right to contraceptives to minors in *Carey v. Population Services International* (1977), reasoning that state laws banning the sale of contraceptive devices to minors violate their right to privacy. A few years later in *Bellotti v. Baird* (1979), the Court held that a parental-consent restriction on minors' abortions is constitutional as long as there is an option for the minor to obtain permission from a court, through a judicial bypass alternative.

There have been no major Supreme Court cases on minors' access to health care except for the above cases regarding contraception and abortion, but many states have recognized a so-called mature minor exception to the general rule of requiring parental consent for the medical treatment of a minor. The mature minor exception relies on making individual decisions about minors based on factors such as age, experience, judgment, and conduct.

Although emancipation gives minors most of the rights of adults, certain rights are not granted at the age of majority. For emancipated eighteen-year-olds, there is no right to drink alcohol for three more years. In addition, there are certain positions that are not open to anyone until a certain age—for example, a person must be at least thirty-five to become president. In contrast to situations where emancipation is not sufficient for certain rights, prior to the age of majority minors may reach the age of criminal responsibility and be tried in court as adults. In addition, most states set the age of consent—or age at which a person is deemed legally competent to consent to sexual acts—prior to the age of majority.

The issue of minor emancipation and the related issues of the age of majority, the drinking age, and the age of consent are fascinating partly because young people achieve different rights at different ages. The exceptions to rights given at emancipation and the ability to achieve partial or full emancipation prior to the age of majority create interesting issues for debate. These issues are explained and explored through relevant court cases and commentary in *Teen Rights and Freedoms: Emancipation*.

Chronology

1944   In *Prince v. Massachusetts* the US
Supreme Court holds that paren-
tal authority is not absolute and the
government has broad authority to
regulate the actions and treatment of
children.

1967   In *Smith v. Seibly* the Supreme Court of
Washington determines that minors, if
mature, may make medical decisions
for themselves.

1971   The Twenty-Sixth Amendment to the
US Constitution is passed, prohibiting
the states and the federal government
from setting the voting age higher than
eighteen years of age.

1975   In *Stanton v. Stanton* the Supreme
Court rules that the age of majority—
the age at which a minor is considered
an adult under the law—must be the
same for males and females.

1976   In *Planned Parenthood of Central
Missouri v. Danforth* the Supreme
Court holds that states may not require
parental consent for a minor's abortion without any exceptions, striking
down one of many abortion restrictions
implemented by Missouri.

1977	In *Carey v. Population Services International* the Supreme Court rules that the rights to privacy and intimate association identified in *Griswold v. Connecticut* (1965) also extend to minors, protecting their rights to access contraceptives.
1979	In *Parham v. J.R.* the Supreme Court determines that parents usually have the authority to make decisions for their children, including the decision to have the child committed to a psychiatric hospital.
1979	In *Bellotti v. Baird* the Supreme Court rules that parental consent for a minor's abortion can be required as long as there is the alternative for a judicial bypass granting permission.
1983	In *Akron v. Akron Center for Reproductive Health, Inc.* the Supreme Court determines, among other things, that it is unconstitutional for a state to determine that all minors under the age of fifteen are too immature to make an abortion decision without parental approval.
1987	In *Cardwell v. Bechtol* the Supreme Court of Tennessee finds that medical treatment may be provided without parental consent to mature minors.

1989   In *In re E.G.* the Supreme Court of Illinois finds that there is a constitutional basis for allowing certain mature minors to refuse medical treatment.

1990   In *Hodgson v. Minnesota* the Supreme Court holds that a two-parent notice requirement for abortion is unconstitutional without a judicial bypass procedure.

1992   In *Belcher v. Charleston Area Med. Center* the Supreme Court of Appeals of West Virginia holds that a physician must obtain parental consent prior to treating a minor, but a mature minor's consent may sometimes override parents' wishes.

> *"Taken together laws for children expressed the persistent conviction of legal policy makers that minors were a special class of citizens who required a different set of legal policies than adults."*

The Evolving Legal Rights of Children Have Always Been Dependent on Age

Michael Grossberg

In the following viewpoint, Michael Grossberg argues that the legal status of children in the United States has drastically changed since the country's founding. Grossberg notes that in early colonial times, children had very few rights, whereas by the end of the twentieth century, a children's rights movement had resulted in many legal rights for minors. Nonetheless, Grossberg claims that what has not changed over the years is the fact that the dividing line between child and adult has always been determined by age, deemed the age of majority. Grossberg is a professor in the Department of History and the School of Law at Indiana University, Bloomington.

As British colonists began peopling North America, political philosopher Thomas Hobbes voiced the stark traditional English view of the legal status of children: "For the child like

Michael Grossberg, "Children and the Law," *Encyclopedia of Children and Childhood*, first edition, Paula S. Fass, ed. New York: Macmillan Reference USA, 2004. Copyright © 2004 Cengage Learning.

the imbecile and the crazed beast there is no law." Over three hundred years later, United States Supreme Court Justice Harry Blackmun reached a very different conclusion. In a decision that granted a minor the right to an abortion without parental consent, Blackmun asserted: "Constitutional rights do not mature and come into being magically only when one attains the state-defined age of majority. Minors, as well as adults, are protected by the Constitution and possess constitutional rights." In the years between these dramatically different declarations, age had become increasingly significant in American law. However, the legal status of children had not simply improved steadily over that time. More critically, the law increasingly had become a primary source of identity, status, and power for American children. It did so as children gradually acquired a separate and distinct legal identity.

The Line Between Child and Adult

Central to the creation of law for children at any particular time and over time has been the ideal of youthful dependence. Though exact conceptions of youthful dependence have changed significantly since the first colonial settlements, in every era of the American past children were assumed to be less competent and more vulnerable than adults. Since immaturity was assumed to render them incapable of making competent decisions about critical aspects of their lives, lawmakers concluded that children should not be as legally accountable as adults for their market, criminal, or other acts. Denying children the legal powers and liabilities of adults also meant that the law entrusted parents, the state, and other adults with significant legal authority over them. Consequently, the line between child and adult became the most critical legal boundary for young Americans. It has been, though, an uncertain marker because of the diversity of American children. Within the legal category of minors, children varied according to age, race, gender, capacity, and other critical factors and these variations complicated legal policies.

Since the seventeenth century, the law dealt with this reality by devising particular policies for particular actions by particular groups of children. Thus, for instance, within the larger legal category of children, minors of various ages have had the legal power to wed before reaching majority. Taken together laws for children expressed the persistent conviction of legal policy makers that minors were a special class of citizens who required a different set of legal policies than adults.

Colonial Americans created a foundation for the law by transferring English policies to their new settlements. Fundamental changes then occurred in the first part of the nineteenth century when a comprehensive code for children was first devised. Other significant changes were made in the late nineteenth and early twentieth centuries when the role of the state in children's lives was increased in significant ways. A second era of substantive change occurred late in the twentieth century. The result of these eras of legal change is a multilayered set of judicial decisions, statutes, and legal customs that has made the law more and more consequential in the lives of American children.

Childhood in Early America

Although never as completely outside of the bounds of law as Hobbes's declaration suggests, children in early America did find themselves enmeshed in a traditional European legal order. Children were part of a patriarchal system in which the household was to replicate the larger polity. Thus the father, like the king, served as head of the family while the wife and children were classified as subordinates. And in an era in which the definition of childhood meant that infants were treated as a distinct group but other children were considered more as members of the adult world, early integration of the young into the larger social order was the primary object of the law. In this system children were bound to their families and communities through webs of reciprocal duties and responsibilities, many of which were codified and enforced through the law. The most profound

The Dilemma for Children's Rights Advocates

The U.S. legal system grants rights to people who are deemed competent to exercise those rights. This qualification poses a dilemma for advocates of children's rights because most children lack the skills to advocate for themselves in the political, judicial, or economic arena. Yet, children's rights supporters believe that because of this powerlessness, children must be granted more protections and power than has been provided in their legal status.

"Children's Rights," West's Encyclopedia of American Law, *second ed., eds. Shirelle Phelps and Jeffrey Lehman. Detroit, MI: Gale 2005.*

of these relationships fell under the traditional doctrine or legal rule of *parens patriae*, which made the monarch or the state the principal protector of children and other dependents. It was, and continues to be, the fundamental legal basis for all state intervention on behalf of children.

Colonial legislatures transferred the English legal system and its fundamental assumptions and policies about the young to the New World with relatively few changes. At its heart was the notion of legal reciprocity: children exchanged their labor for parental care. Parents, primarily fathers, assumed the responsibility to maintain and educate their offspring and to give them a suitable start in life. In exchange, fathers were granted the right to the custody of their children and in turn the right to a child's labor. Mothers had relatively few legal rights to their children's custody or labor. Equally important, the imposition of English rules governing the age of majority made it the primary legal dividing line between children and adults. Set according to English custom at twenty-one, the age of majority was the designated point at which a youth shed the disabilities of childhood and assumed the full rights and responsibilities of adulthood.

Majority marked off childhood as a distinct legal category and made children legal dependents, but it could not encapsulate all youthful legal actions. Instead, the law crafted rules for specific actions, such as the right of girls to wed at twelve and boys at fourteen or the criminal innocence of children under the age of seven. In this way, following English policies meant establishing both a clear legal line between children and adults and also secondary lines within childhood for particular legal acts. This combination of uniformity and specificity laid the basis for the legal treatment of American children well into the future. It also ensured that legal contests would be waged over what a minor could or should be able to do and what he or she could not or should not do. . . .

Colonial legal policies represented a transatlantic transfer of traditional European policies codifying the dependent status of the youth. They were premised on the belief that child welfare was best promoted by the creation of webs of reciprocity that made families and, when they failed, communities responsible for children. In exchange, both were given extensive rights to govern the young. Policies like the age of majority established a European base for laws that would continue to govern children's lives far into the future. In this regime, children had few independent legal rights or powers and age was relatively unimportant as a source of distinctive legal rules. Thus in many ways the law was simply less significant in the lives of colonial children than it would be for later generations.

The Place of Children After the Revolution

In the years after the American Revolution, the laws governing children were transformed in fundamental ways. Legal change was both a cause and a product of larger changes in the place of children in American society. New family beliefs and practices treated children more than ever before as distinct individuals with special needs. An individualization of the household implicit in the new view of the family led to an understanding of children as particular kinds of people with distinct rights and duties and relationships with the state. Age became a more important demarcation of legal rights and responsibilities, a development that challenged the Hobbesian view of children as beyond the reach of the law.

Determining a new legal place for the young became a major challenge for the antebellum legal order. It was one addressed primarily in the states because under reigning American conceptions of federalism the states had primary jurisdiction over children and families. As the principal definers of children's legal status, state judges and legislators struggled to find a way to treat children somehow as distinct individuals and yet not adults in a system that tied legal power to individual autonomy. The result was to emphasize children's needs. This approach found its most revealing expression in a new doctrine that would dominate legal debates about children into the twenty-first century: *the best interests of the child.* Early in the nineteenth century, judges and other policy makers developed this doctrine by reinterpreting the *parens patriae* power of the state to include a newfound sense of children as having distinct interests recognizable by the law. The legal doctrine contained the assumption that children had their own needs and that others, most appropriately parents, and when they failed, judges or other suitable public or private officials such as the overseers of the poor, must determine them. At the same time, this doctrine supported the emerging notion of the family as a private institution that should be granted significant autonomy by deferring to family privacy and parental rights. In this way, the new rule sanctioned broad discretionary authority to determine the interests of children only in the event of family conflict or failure. . . .

The legal place of American children was transformed during the years between the Revolution and the Civil War. The new laws expressed rules and assumptions of a legal order more explicitly stratified by age than ever before. They made the primary line between adulthood and childhood even more of a legal divider between rights and needs, autonomy and dependence. Children, like other dependents in a society fundamentally divided by class, race, and gender, were designated special legal individuals, and the legal officials created special policies like these for them. As childhood came to constitute a separate legal category, the law moved further from the Hobbesian view of youthful legal powerlessness.

The Development of Children's Rights

In the turbulent years after the Civil War, the law regarding children underwent further change as it was selectively re-drawn to include a greater role for state regulation of the young. A new assertion of public power and public interest in families challenged the now powerful American tradition of family autonomy: the right of families to be left alone and of parents to raise their children as they saw fit. That challenge was prompted by a growing sense among the middle and upper classes that families were in crisis. Beginning in the 1870s, fears about disordered families stirred an intense national debate about the fate of children. Concern about abuse, delinquency, and neglect led to demands for greater state intervention based on the *parens patriae* doctrine. The resulting expansion of the role of the state in children's lives also expressed a growing faith in law as a tool for changing children's lives.

Self-styled child-savers took the lead in extending youthful dependence as they and their legislative allies filled states' codes with new regulations that substantially enlarged the legal definition of risks facing children. Each addition, from bans on entering dance halls or skating rinks and prohibitions against joining the circus or purchasing alcohol, to specific criminal penalties against child abuse or neglect, represented a risk that now had to be prescribed. Each was premised on the assumption that childhood was a distinctive and vulnerable stage of life and that public regulation of child rearing had to be expanded to protect the young. These assumptions in turn were drawn in part from a new conviction that older children should be more precisely segregated into their own legal category of adolescence. Much of the debate and controversy of the era focused on this newly designated group of children and the determination that their childhood must be prolonged by keeping them in their families to gain more extensive preparation for adult roles. The intent, if not the full result, of changes like these was to use the law to increase children's dependence on adults and to remove the young from the adult spheres of the marketplace and the civic community. This logic was evident in the successful campaign to raise the legal age of marriage from the old common-law standards of twelve for girls and fourteen for boys to sixteen and eighteen respectively. Protective legislation like this also challenged an earlier faith in parental supervision of their offspring by circumscribing parental authority and creating a more direct legal relationship between children and the state. . . .

The most radical departure of the era was the creation of a special set of legal rights for children. Devising rights for children proved difficult because the existing concept of rights was designed only for adults who could assert their own claims directly against the state. Children could not do this, nor did reformers want them to. Instead they fashioned an idea of paternalistic rights that defined children's rights in special age-bound terms of needs and parental failure instead of the individual autonomy associated with adult legal rights. Reformers did so by recasting education, socialization, nurture, and other fundamental needs of children as rights. In this way children's rights acquired a restrictive meaning. Children did at times assert more adult-like rights. Newsboys, for instance, organized a successful strike against New York press magnets based on their belief in their rights as workers. And sons and daughters used the juvenile court to renegotiate authority within their families by seizing the

President Nixon signs the Twenty-Sixth Amendment to the US Constitution, giving eighteen-year-olds the right to vote and redefining the civic rights of adolescents in 1971. © Bettmann/Corbis/Associated Press.

right to lodge complaints against abusive parents. Nevertheless, in most cases it was not children, but parents, reformers, or bureaucrats who asserted the newly proclaimed children's rights. For example, United States Supreme Court decisions in the 1920s such as *Meyer v. Nebraska* (1923) and *Pierce v. Society of Sisters* (1925) used children's rights to schooling to construct a constitutional foundation for parents' control of their children's education. Thus the initial conception of children's legal rights was steeped in paternalism; it translated children's needs into rights without jettisoning their dependent status. Such rights were unusual because they could not be exercised or waived by their holder. In this way, paternalistic rights institutionalized the irresolvable tension between treating the young as family dependents or as autonomous individuals.

In this era, most legal policies for the young devised in the previous period remained in place, but revisions used the law to increase the presence of the state in children's lives and to create a more direct relationship between children and the state. The result was greater legal surveillance of children and yet also the emergence of the first legal rights for young Americans. These two seemingly contradictory developments suggest both the depth and significance of the legal developments of the era.

An Era of Legal Changes

The law regarding children took another dramatic turn in the last half of the twentieth century. Basic legal rules and practices underwent enough changes to warrant comparisons with the transformations of the early nineteenth century. At the core of the era's changes were two new realities. First, the federal government, and particularly the federal courts, assumed a powerful role in setting legal policies for America's young people. Consequently, many of the endemic tensions in American law that had plagued state lawmakers in the nineteenth century began to bedevil federal lawmakers in the twentieth. Second, rights for children underwent a major redefinition. In an era dominated by rights struggles, children's legal rights became a movement. For the first time children's plight in America was explained as a consequence of the lack of adult rights: an assertion challenging the long-standing belief that the denial of adult rights to children required no justification. The impact of the twin developments was evident in almost every legal category as the laws governing children moved even further from their Hobbesian roots. . . .

Statutory changes, judicial decisions, and even a constitutional amendment significantly increased juvenile rights, particularly for adolescents. The federal courts, especially the Supreme Court, played a key role in recasting children's rights. Since the 1930s the courts had been increasingly receptive to claims of individual liberty and due process rights. They applied those concerns to children beginning in 1954 with *Brown v. Board of Education*. The unanimous decision not only declared segregated schools unconstitutional, but it presented the ruling in terms of children's rights: "In these days it is doubtful that any child may reasonably be expected to succeed in life if he is denied the opportunity of an education. Such an opportunity, where the state has undertaken to provide it, is a right which must be made available to all children." Children's rights expanded further in a series of cases that gave children constitutionally protected rights they could assert against the state and even against their parents. *In re Gault* (1967) granted youths coming before juvenile courts procedural rights such as the right to counsel and thus restored some of the rights lost when the juvenile courts had been created. *Tinker v. Des Moines* (1969) ruled that high school students had the constitutional right to freedom of speech. Decisions like these applied adult models of rights to children. And those rights were increased by corresponding statutory changes such as medical emancipation laws and lowered drinking ages. Finally, the Twenty-Sixth Amendment lowered the voting age to eighteen and thus redefined the civic rights of adolescents. Tellingly, "age-blind" rights became the goal of children's rights advocates, who argued that children should have the same rights as adults. Indeed, some even called for the abolition of minority status, which was likened to slavery and coverture.

However, the legal changes of the era did not eliminate the use of age as a means of determining legal rights. Instead resistance arose to the notion of autonomous children's rights and thus renewed the debate over the legal status of the young. Even the Supreme Court consistently qualified its assertions of children's rights. In *Tinker* Justice Potter Stewart had insisted that the rights of children were not "co-extensive with those of adults." And in *Ginsburg v. New York* (1968) the court upheld limits on access to obscene materials to those over seventeen, with one justice declaring: "I think that a State may permissibly determine that, at least in some precisely delineated areas, a child—like someone in a captive audience—is not possessed of that full capacity for individual choice which is the presupposition of First Amendment guarantees." Such caveats underscored the persistence of legal policies that assumed the dependent status of children and the paternal power of the state. And amid fears of mounting risks to the young—parental abuse, teen pregnancy, suicide, drug addiction, gang membership—the children's rights movement itself faced growing opposition. Critics argued that more rights put children at risk instead of helping them. They challenged the premise that autonomous adult rights were the most effective means of raising and resolving children's problems. Indeed a growing number of opponents charged that increased rights had undermined child welfare by fostering adversarial family relations and undermining necessary parental and school authority.

These concerns led to another round of legal change in the last decades of the twentieth century. States began to revise some of their earlier endorsements of greater rights for children. For instance, Michigan, which in 1971 had lowered the minimum age for purchasing alcoholic beverages from twenty-one to eighteen, raised the age back up to twenty-one seven years later. Similarly, state legislators sought to impose greater restrictions on the right of young women to obtain abortions without parental consent. And in response to increases in violent juvenile crime, states rejected rehabilitation in favor of policies that made it easier for prosecutors to try adolescents who commit serious crimes as adults and to sentence them to adult prisons. Doing so erased not only rights but previous protections that resulted from age-defined dependency. . . .

In 1993, the Illinois Appellate Court offered its reading of the history of children and the law in the United States. The judges declared: "Fortunately, the time has long past when children in our society were considered the property of their parents. Slowly, but finally, when it comes to children even the law rid itself of the Dred Scott mentality that a human being can be considered a piece of property 'belonging' to another human being. To hold that a child is the property of his parents is to deny the humanity of the child." This judicial declaration certainly captured a part of that history, particularly the growth of distinctive laws and especially legal rights for the young. And it suggests how fundamental the legal changes have been since Hobbes placed the young beyond the law. However, the progressive vision of constant improvement in the legal condition of children masks the persistence of conflict and controversy and ignores the complicated relationship between children and the law. Greater legal autonomy for American children has not always meant better lives or even recognition of their humanity, though it has meant the law assumed a greater and greater presence in the lives of children. Consequently, at the dawn of the twenty-first century age continues to be a fundamental dividing line in the law. And that will surely be the case in the future as well.

> "We perceive nothing rational in the
> distinction drawn by § 15-2-1 which,
> when related to the divorce decree,
> results in the appellee's liability for
> support for Sherri only to age 18 but
> for Rick to age 21."

The Age of Majority Must Be the Same for Males and Females

The Supreme Court's Decision

Harry Blackmun

In the following viewpoint Harry Blackmun, writing for the majority of the US Supreme Court, finds that a Utah law setting the age of majority for females at eighteen years of age and for males at twenty-one years of age violates the Equal Protection Clause of the US Constitution. Blackmun determines that Utah provides no reasonable state interest in support of the law, reasoning that the law is based on outdated ideas about the differences between males and females. Blackmun concludes that the state may determine the age of majority as it sees fit, but that the same age must apply to both males and females. Blackmun served as associate justice of the Supreme Court from 1970 until 1994.

This case presents the issue whether a state statute specifying for males a greater age of majority than it specifies for

Harry Blackmun, Majority opinion, *Stanton v. Stanton*, US Supreme Court, April 15, 1975.

females denies, in the context of a parent's obligation for support payments for his children, the equal protection of the laws guaranteed by § 1 of the Fourteenth Amendment.

Age of Majority by Gender

Appellant Thelma B. Stanton and appellee James Lawrence Stanton, Jr., were married at Elko, Nev., in February 1951. At the suit of the appellant, they were divorced in Utah on November 29, 1960. They have a daughter, Sherri Lyn, born in February 1953, and a son, Rick Arlund, born in January 1955. Sherri became 18 on February 12, 1971, and Rick on January 29, 1973.

During the divorce proceedings in the District Court of Salt Lake County, the parties entered into a stipulation as to property, child support, and alimony. The court awarded custody of the children to their mother and incorporated provisions of the stipulation into its findings and conclusions and into its decree of divorce. Specifically, as to alimony and child support, the decree provided:

"Defendant is ordered to pay to plaintiff the sum of $300.00 per month as child support and alimony, $100.00 per month for each child as child support and $100.00 per month as alimony, to be paid on or before the 1st day of each month through the office of the Salt Lake County Clerk."

The appellant thereafter remarried; the court, pursuant to another stipulation, then modified the decree to relieve the appellee from payment of further alimony. The appellee also later remarried.

When Sherri attained 18 the appellee discontinued payments for her support. In May 1973 the appellant moved the divorce court for entry of judgment in her favor and against the appellee for, among other things, support for the children for the periods after each respectively attained the age of 18 years. The court concluded that on February 12, 1971, Sherri "became 18 years of age, and under the provisions of [§] 15-2-1 Utah Code Annotated 1953, thereby attained her majority. Defendant is not obligated

In Stanton v. Stanton *(1975), the US Supreme Court ruled that the age of majority must be the same for men and women.* © iStock.com/track 5.

to plaintiff for maintenance and support of Sherri Lyn Stanton since that date." An order denying the appellant's motion was entered accordingly.

The appellant appealed to the Supreme Court of Utah. She contended, among other things, that Utah Code Ann. § 15-2-1 (1953) to the effect that the period of minority for males extends to age 21 and for females to age 18, is invidiously discriminatory and serves to deny due process and equal protection of the laws, in violation of the Fourteenth Amendment and of the corresponding provisions of the Utah Constitution. On this issue, the Utah court affirmed. The court acknowledged: "There is no doubt that the questioned statute treats men and women differently," but said that people may be treated differently "so long as there is a reasonable basis for the classification, which is related to the purposes of the act, and it applies equally and uniformly to all persons within the class." The court referred to what it called some "old notions," namely, "that generally it is the man's primary responsibility to provide a home and its essentials"; that "it is a salutary thing for him to get a good education and/or training before he undertakes those responsibilities"; that "girls tend generally to mature physically, emotionally and mentally before boys"; and that "they generally tend to marry earlier." It concluded:

> [I]t is our judgment that there is no basis upon which we would be justified in concluding that the statute is so beyond a reasonable doubt in conflict with constitutional provisions that it should be stricken down as invalid.

If such a change were desirable, the court said, "that is a matter which should commend itself to the attention of the legislature." The appellant, thus, was held not entitled to support for Sherri for the period after she attained 18, but was entitled to support for Rick "during his minority" unless otherwise ordered by the trial court. . . .

The Equal Protection Clause

The appellant argues that Utah's statutory prescription establishing different ages of majority for males and females denies equal protection; that it is a classification based solely on sex and affects a child's "fundamental right" to be fed, clothed, and sheltered by its parents; that no compelling state interest supports the classification; and that the statute can withstand no judicial scrutiny, "close" or otherwise, for it has no relationship to any ascertainable legislative objective. The appellee contends that the test is that of rationality and that the age classification has a rational basis and endures any attack based on equal protection.

We find it unnecessary in this case to decide whether a classification based on sex is inherently suspect.

Reed [*v. Reed* (1971)], we feel, is controlling here. That case presented an equal protection challenge to a provision of the Idaho probate code which gave preference to males over females when persons otherwise of the same entitlement applied for appointment as administrator of a decedent's estate. No regard was paid under the statute to the applicants' respective individual qualifications. In upholding the challenge, the Court reasoned that the Idaho statute accorded different treatment on the basis of sex and that it "thus establishes a classification subject to scrutiny under the Equal Protection Clause." The Clause, it was said, denies to States "the power to legislate that different treatment be accorded to persons placed by a statute into different classes on the basis of criteria wholly unrelated to the objective of that statute." "A classification must be reasonable, not arbitrary, and must rest upon some ground of difference having a fair and substantial relation to the object of the legislation, so that all persons similarly circumstanced shall be treated alike." It was not enough to save the statute that among its objectives were the elimination both of an area of possible family controversy and of a hearing on the comparative merits of petitioning relatives.

The test here, then, is whether the difference in sex between children warrants the distinction in the appellee's obligation to support that is drawn by the Utah statute. We conclude that it does not. It may be true, as the Utah court observed and as is argued here, that it is the man's primary responsibility to provide a home and that it is salutary for him to have education and training before he assumes that responsibility; that girls tend to mature earlier than boys; and that females tend to marry earlier than males. The last mentioned factor, however, under the Utah statute loses whatever weight it otherwise might have, for the statute states that "all minors obtain their majority by marriage"; thus minority, and all that goes with it, is abruptly lost by marriage of a person of either sex at whatever tender age the marriage occurs.

Utah's Age of Majority Law

Prior to *Stanton v. Stanton* (1975)

> "15-2-1. Period of minority. The period of minority extends in males to the age of 21 years and in females to that of 18 years; but all minors obtain their majority by marriage."

After the US Supreme Court's *Stanton v. Stanton* decision the Utah Legislature amended the statute to read:

> "15-2-1. Period of minority. The period of minority extends in males and females to the age of 18 years; but all minors obtain their majority by marriage. It is further provided that courts in divorce actions may order support to age 21."

Utah Code, Title 15, Chapter 2, Section 1, amended by Chapter 39, 1975 General Session.

The State's Justification for the Distinction

Notwithstanding the "old notions" to which the Utah court referred, we perceive nothing rational in the distinction drawn by § 15-2-1 which, when related to the divorce decree, results in the appellee's liability for support for Sherri only to age 18 but for Rick to age 21. This imposes "criteria wholly unrelated to the objective of that statute." A child, male or female, is still a child. No longer is the female destined solely for the home and the rearing of the family, and only the male for the marketplace and the world of ideas. Women's activities and responsibilities are increasing and expanding. Coeducation is a fact, not a rarity. The presence of women in business, in the professions, in government and, indeed, in all walks of life where education is a desirable, if not always a necessary, antecedent is apparent and a proper subject of judicial notice. If a specified age of minority is required for the boy in order to assure him parental support while he attains his education and training, so, too, is it for the girl. To distinguish between the two on educational grounds is to be self-serving: if the female is not to be supported so long as the male, she hardly can be expected to attend school as long as he does, and bringing her education to an end earlier coincides with the role-typing society has long imposed. And if any weight remains in this day to the claim of earlier maturity of the female, with a concomitant inference of absence of need for support beyond 18, we fail to perceive its unquestioned truth or its significance, particularly when marriage, as the statute provides, terminates minority for a person of either sex.

Only Arkansas, as far as our investigation reveals, remains with Utah in fixing the age of majority for females at 18 and for males at 21. Furthermore, Utah itself draws the 18–21 distinction only in § 15-2-1 defining minority, and in § 30-1-9 relating to marriage without the consent of parent or guardian. Elsewhere, in the State's present constitutional and statutory structure, the male and the female appear to be treated alike. The State's Constitution provides that the rights of Utah citizens to vote and hold office "shall not be denied or abridged on account of sex," and that "[b]oth male and female citizens . . . shall enjoy equally all civil, political and religious rights and privileges," and, since long before the Nation's adoption of the Twenty-sixth Amendment in 1971, did provide that every citizen "of the age of twenty-one years and upwards," who satisfies durational requirements, "shall be entitled to vote." Utah's statutes provide that any citizen over the age of 21 who meets specified nonsex qualifications is "competent to act as a juror," may be admitted to the practice of law, and may act as an incorporator, and, if under 21 and in need, may be entitled to public assistance. The ages at which persons may serve in legislative, executive, and judicial offices are the same for males and females. Tobacco may not be sold, purchased, or possessed by persons of either sex under 19 years of age. No age differential is imposed with respect to the issuance of motor vehicle licenses. State adult education programs are open to every person 18 years of age or over. The Uniform Gifts to Minors Act is in effect in Utah and defines a minor, for its purposes, as any person "who has not attained the age of twenty-one years." Juvenile court jurisdiction extends to persons of either sex under a designated age. Every person over the age of 18 and of sound mind may dispose of his property by will. And the Uniform Civil Liability for Support Act, noted above and in effect in Utah since 1957, imposes on each parent an obligation of support of both sons and daughters until age 21.

This is not to say that § 15-2-1 does not have important effect in application. A "minor" may disaffirm his contracts. An "infant" must appear in court by guardian or guardian *ad litem*. A parent has a right of action for injury to, or wrongful death of, "a minor child." A person "[u]nder the age of majority" is not competent or entitled to serve as an administrator of a decedent's estate, or as the executor of a decedent's will. The statute of limitations is tolled while a person entitled to bring an action is "[u]nder the age of majority." Thus, the distinction drawn by § 15-2-1 affects other rights and duties. It has pervasive effect, both direct and collateral.

The Court's Conclusion

We therefore conclude that under any test—compelling state interest, or rational basis, or something in between—§ 15-2-1, in the context of child support, does not survive an equal protection attack. In that context, no valid distinction between male and female may be drawn.

Our conclusion that in the context of child support the classification effectuated by § 15-2-1 denies the equal protection of the laws, as guaranteed by the Fourteenth Amendment, does not finally resolve the controversy as between this appellant and this appellee. With the age differential held invalid, it is not for this Court to determine *when* the appellee's obligation for his children's support, pursuant to the divorce decree, terminates under Utah law. The appellant asserts that, with the classification eliminated, the common law applies and that at common law the age of majority for both males and females is 21. The appellee claims that any unconstitutional inequality between males and females is to be remedied by treating males as adults at age 18, rather than by withholding the privileges of adulthood from women until they reach 21. This plainly is an issue of state law to be resolved by the Utah courts on remand.

> "State law can allow a minor to ask a state court to determine that the minor is able to assume adult responsibilities before reaching the age of majority."

The Requirements for Minor Emancipation Vary by State

Gale Encyclopedia of Everyday Law

In the following viewpoint, the author argues that the emancipation of minors is automatic at the age of majority, at which time the minor assumes all responsibilities of adulthood. The author contends that other events that occur prior to the age of majority, such as joining the armed forces, can result in emancipation. The author claims that approximately half the states maintain laws that allow minors to petition the court for emancipation prior to the age of majority, but in these states there are requirements that minors must meet in order to have their petitions granted, such as showing the ability to be financially independent and meet basic needs.

Historically, parents are responsible for their children. They are also required to feed, clothe, educate, and act in their children's best interest until they reach the "age of majority" or the age in which, for most purposes, the children are considered to be adults. State law can allow a minor to ask a state court to

"Emancipation," *Americans with Disabilities Act to Family Law*, from *Gale Encyclopedia of Everyday Law*, third edition, Donna Batten, ed. Detroit: Gale, 2013, pp. 713–716. Copyright © 2013 Cengage Learning.

determine that the minor is able to assume adult responsibilities before reaching the age of majority. The term emancipation refers to the point at which a minor becomes self-supporting, assumes adult responsibility for his or her welfare, and is no longer under the care of his or her parents. Upon achieving emancipation, the minor thereby assumes the rights, privileges, and duties of adulthood before actually reaching the "age of majority" (adulthood). At that point, the minor's parents are no longer responsible for that child and, also, have no claim to the minor's earnings. During the court proceedings and before granting emancipation, the court considers, primarily, the best interests and level of maturity of the minor and confirms that the minor is able to financially support him or herself.

However, even when minors achieve emancipation, they cannot take part in any activity such as purchasing and/or drinking alcohol, voting, or getting married which, by statute, may require that the participant have attained an older age.

The Requirements for Emancipation

Close to half of the states, including New York and Pennsylvania, provide no separate statutory provisions for emancipation. Instead, these states rely on the fact that emancipation is automatically achieved upon a minor getting married, joining the armed forces, or reaching the age of majority which is now lower (usually eighteen years of age) than what was once commonly mandated as 21 years of age.

Generally, the statutory age in which a minor can petition a court for emancipation is at least 16 years or older but below the age of majority (which among the vast majority of states is eighteen years of age). California allows a minor of the age of 14 to petition its courts for emancipation.

Even though minors may be under the age of majority, certain actions on their part will cause them to be emancipated from their parents' care and control even without seeking a court order. These actions are usually limited to the following:

- Joining the armed forces
- Getting married
- Reaching the actual age of majority (which is 18 years of age in most states)

The state of Michigan also allows for a temporary automatic emancipation when minors are in police custody and emergency medical care is required. The minors are considered emancipated and allowed to consent to such care. This emancipation ends when the medical care or treatment is completed.

Emancipation Through the Courts

Minors petitioning their state courts for emancipation from their parents' care and control are normally required to prove their age and that they are residents of the state where the petition is being filed. They must tell the court why they seek emancipation. Parents must be given notice of the proceeding. Also, the minors must show the court that they are of sufficient maturity to care for themselves. This means that they are able to support themselves financially, provide for their own shelter, and make decisions on their own behalf. Some states require that the minors already support themselves and live totally or partially on their own. Most statutes exclude state financial support or "general assistance" when determining minors' ability to support themselves.

The court then looks at all the evidence in order to determine whether emancipation is in the minor's best interest. Also, since an order for emancipation must be in the minor's best interest, if the minor's situation changes, such an order may be rescinded by the court and the minor declared to be returned to the parents' care and control. The state of Illinois allows for court decrees of "partial" emancipation, where the court clearly states the limits of emancipation, if such an order is in the best interests of the minor.

States with no statutory provision or procedures for minors to apply for emancipation may still determine or confirm that

THE AGE OF MAJORITY BY STATE

18   19   21

minors have been emancipated. Minors file a petition with the court and provide the information necessary (such as proof of financial independence, adequate housing arrangements, and sufficient maturity) for the court to determine that such a confirmation of emancipation from parental care and control is in the best interests of the minor.

Criteria for and Rights of Emancipation

Criteria for determining whether a decree declaring *emancipation is in the minor's best interest vary among* the states. However, certain criteria can commonly be found:

- The minors' ability to support themselves financially, either currently or in the future
- The minors are currently living apart from their parents or have made adequate arrangements for future housing
- The minors can adequately make decisions for themselves
- The minors are attending school or have already received a diploma
- The minors exhibit sufficient maturity to function as adults

Once declared to be emancipated, minors have the same rights, privileges, and duties in society as adults. Although the specific aspects vary among the states, generally, emancipated minors can do the following:

- Enter into contracts and leases
- Be a party to a lawsuit, either as a plaintiff or a defendant, in their own name
- Buy or sell real estate or other property
- Write a valid will
- Inherit property
- Enroll in school
- Get married
- Agree to various types of medical treatments

Emancipated minors can also vote and obtain a driver's license but only if they are of sufficient age to do so.

State Provisions on Emancipation

Of the states with specific emancipation provisions, some of the more significant state requirements include the following:

Alabama In Alabama, the age of majority is 19. The Alabama code describing the emancipation procedure is designed to expand the rights of minors over the age of 18 but under the age of majority. Parents can file an emancipation petition with the court or the minor seeking emancipation can file the petition if that minor has no parents or if a living parent is insane or has abandoned the minor. The court will then decide if a decree of emancipation is in the "interest of such minor."

California In California, the age of majority is 18. Minors are considered emancipated without court intervention if they are married, are a member of the armed forces, or have previously been declared emancipated by a California court. Otherwise, in order to seek court mandated emancipation, the minors must be no younger than fourteen years old, be already living apart from their parents, be able to demonstrate the ability to take adequate care of themselves financially, and not receive any income from illegal or criminal activity.

If the court grants the order of emancipation, the minor then has the privilege and right to: sign contracts; approve medical care; buy, lease, and sell real property; be the plaintiff or defendant in a lawsuit; write a will; live in their own home; go to school; and get a work permit. If the minor's situation changes, the court has the ability to end the emancipation and advise the minor's parents that they are once again responsible for the minor.

Florida The age of majority in Florida is 18. In order to seek a court mandated emancipation, minors must submit a statement of "character, habits, income, and mental capacity for business, and an explanation of how the needs of the minor with respect to food, shelter, clothing, medical care, and other necessities will be met." In addition, minors must state whether they are party to any court action taking place in Florida or another state. Minors must also submit a statement explaining why they seek an order of emancipation. Parents must be notified of any such proceeding.

The court then asks for any additional evidence to determine if the decree of emancipation is in the minors' best interest. If the order of emancipation is granted, the minor will have all of the

Marriage is one way for minors to gain emancipation without seeking a court order. © iStock
.com/TriggerPhoto.

rights, responsibilities, and privileges of anyone who has reached
the age of majority (18 years of age).

Illinois: The age of majority in Illinois is 18. The Illinois statute allows the court to give an order of emancipation to a "mature minor who has demonstrated the ability and capacity to manage his
(or her) own affairs and to live wholly or partially independent
of his (or her) parents." The Illinois statute also seeks to tailor the
content of the emancipation order to fit the needs of the minor
seeking the order.

The statute states that for an order of emancipation from
the court to be valid, neither the parents nor the minor can offer any objections. Also, the court will examine the situation
and determine whether a full or partial order of emancipation
will be given. Also, once the emancipation order is entered, the
court will determine what adult privileges and rights, in addition to the right to enter into contracts, will be given the minor.

Only those rights listed in the order will be in effect for that minor.

In order to seek a court mandated emancipation order, the minor must be at least 16 years old but under 18 years old. The minor must confirm that he or she lives in Illinois, explain why he or she wants a complete or partial order of emancipation, demonstrate that he or she is a "mature minor," and show that he or she has lived on their own.

Massachusetts The age of majority in Massachusetts is 18. There is no formal means for a minor to become emancipated from parents, and most judges will not grant requests. In some rare instances, however, a judge will grant a request when emancipation is in a child's best interests.

In 2009, a state appellate judge ruled that a child does not become emancipated simply by having a child. The court noted that other states have issued similar rulings.

Michigan The age of majority in Michigan is 18. The Michigan statute defines emancipation as the "termination of the rights of the parents to the custody, control, services and earnings of a minor." Absent an order of emancipation, the statute confirms that parents are responsible for supporting their minor children. In fact, one or both parents can object to the emancipation proceedings. In that case, the court may decide to dismiss the proceedings.

The Michigan statute states the four ways that a minor can be emancipated without a court order as being marriage, reaching the age of majority (18 years of age), joining the armed forces, and temporarily while in police custody in order to consent to needed medical treatment.

The statute requires the petition to the court to be brought by the minor. The minors must submit information showing that they can take care of themselves financially, without seeking assistance from the state of Michigan. Minors must also show the court that they can take care of their other personal needs as well. The petition to the court must include a statement from an adult sufficiently familiar with the minor that the individual can offer information that explains to the court why emancipation is "in the best interest of the minor."

At this point, the court may seek additional information and may ask someone from the court staff to investigate the situation further and report back to the court. The court then determines if an order of emancipation is in the minor's best interests.

If the minor is emancipated, the adult rights and responsibilities applicable to the minor do not include those limited by age and by law such as using and purchasing alcohol and voting. However, they do include signing contracts, being a plaintiff or defendant to a lawsuit, keeping whatever money the minor earns, living away from the parents, approving health care and medical procedures, getting married, writing a will, and enrolling in school.

If the minor's circumstances change, the emancipation order can be rescinded by the court. If that happens, the parents "are not liable for any debts incurred by the minor during the period of emancipation."

North Carolina The age of majority in North Carolina is 18. A minor must be at least 16 years of age in order to seek an order of emancipation from the court. The court will consider several factors—including the parents' need for the minor's earnings as well as the minor's ability to accept adult responsibilities—in determining the best interests of the minor.

If the emancipation is granted, the minor will have the adult rights to sign contracts, take part in lawsuits, and conduct other adult-related business. The parents' duties of support to the minor are thereby ended.

Oregon The age of majority in Oregon is 18. A minor must be 16 years of age to seek an order of emancipation from the court.

The minor must show that they can support him or herself and otherwise assume adult responsibilities. If the court determines that an order of emancipation is in the best interests of the minor, then the minor "has all of the rights and is subject to all liabilities of a citizen of full age."

Vermont A minor must be at least 16 years old in order to seek an order of emancipation from the court. Minors are considered to be emancipated without a court order if they are married or have entered the armed forces. In order for the court to consider making an order of emancipation, the minors must have already lived separately from their parents, successfully taken care of their own finances, shown that they can take care of other personal business, either have received a high school diploma or are working toward one, and not be a ward of the social services or corrections department.

Washington A child seeking a court order for emancipation must show the following by clear and convincing evidence: (1) the child is a resident of Washington; (2) the child has the ability to handle financial affairs; (3) the child can handle other affairs, including educational, personal, social, and other affairs; and (4) denying emancipation would harm the child.

West Virginia A minor must be at least 16 years old in order to seek an order of emancipation from the court. Minors must also show the court that they can provide for themselves and their "physical and financial well-being and have the ability to make decisions" for themselves. If an emancipation order is entered, minors have the rights and privileges of adults.

| *"Cases of normal children filing for emancipation from their parents are extremely rare."*

Want to Get Emancipated from Your Parents? Better Be Rich

Eliza Shapiro

In the following viewpoint, Eliza Shapiro argues that although the request for emancipation by child stars is reported frequently in the news, for most minors emancipation is an option of last resort. Shapiro contends that child stars achieve emancipation because of their wealth, but that the trend among average minors is toward requiring care from their parents for more years, not less. Shapiro is a reporter for The Daily Beast, *covering breaking news, crime, and politics.*

Will Smith's son may be able to joke about legally emancipating himself from his famous parents, but for the majority of kids, there's nothing funny about it.

Jaden Smith, who co-stars with his father in the upcoming film *After Earth*, made headlines this week for suggesting that he wanted to divorce his mom and dad so he could have his own home. He was quick to clarify later that he wasn't actually considering making it official. "I'm not going anywhere," he told Ellen DeGeneres.

Good thing—because he wouldn't have been able to buy a house anyway. "Emancipated minors can't buy a home or sign a lease," says Amy Lemley, a lawyer and policy director for the John Burton Foundation, a nonprofit for homeless children. "They can't even rent a car. And you can't work for a wage that will sustain you economically unless you're a child star."

For reasons like this, Lemley says, cases of normal children filing for emancipation from their parents are extremely rare, and the courts discourage it strongly. "Very few juvenile courts will allow a child to even file for emancipation," Lemley says. "Our system is just not set up for emancipated minors." If a child is being abused or mistreated, Lemley says, and they have nowhere to go, they will be removed from their home by Social Services and placed in the foster care system.

Emancipation is considered such a last-resort option that Lemley and Jacqueline Caster, the founder and president of Everychild, a women's philanthropic organization for children, helped pass a bill in California that allows minors in the foster care system to stay put until they're 21 instead of 18, allowing them three more years of being dependents.

Of course, in this respect and in so many others, rich kids are different. In 1996, when *Home Alone* star Macaulay Culkin filed and won emancipation from his parents at age 16, claiming that they had mismanaged his money, he walked away with a $17 million fortune and fabulous career prospects. Likewise, when stars like Alicia Silverstone, Eliza Dushku, and Laura Dern legally extracted themselves from their parents, they were all doing so in order to skirt child-labor laws and work longer hours on the TV shows and movies that were paying them so well.

Macaulay Culkin's wealth and celebrity helped him gain emancipation at age sixteen, which rarely happens with children who don't have the means to support themselves. © Evan Agostini/ImageDirect/Getty Images.

Child Stars Who Obtained Emancipation

Drew Barrymore: Age 15

Macaulay Culkin: Age 16

Laura Dern: Age 13

Eliza Dushku: Age 17

Courtney Love: Age 17

Jena Malone: Age 15

Alicia Silverstone: Age 15

Michelle Williams: Age 15

Drew Barrymore, who had her breakout role at 7 years old in *E.T.* and who was a regular user of cocaine by age 13, emancipated from her actor parents at 15. Though she had a troubled childhood, she had the money and connections to support herself when most others couldn't.

"I did what I had to do to get [emancipated]," Barrymore said during a *60 Minutes* interview, "which was play by the rules and refigure out my life and disconnect myself from the people I knew and the lifestyle I knew and prove that I was a responsible citizen with a good head on my shoulders."

Courtney Love, on the other hand, emancipated herself at age 16, long before she gained fame as a rock star and actress. She worked as a stripper to pay the bills and was able to go to college only with a small trust fund left to her. (In an ironic twist, her daughter with the late Kurt Cobain, Frances Bean, legally emancipated herself from Love in 2011 with a large inheritance that allowed her to pursue a career as a model and artist.)

For everyone who's not famous, Lemley points out that the general trend in the U.S. has been for children to live with their parents farther into adulthood than ever before. Health-care reform has allowed young adults to stay on their parents' health-insurance coverage through age 26, an opportunity thousands have taken advantage of.

Melissa Francis, a former child actress on *Little House on the Prairie*, told Fox she regrets emancipating herself from her parents as a teenager. "I didn't have a driver's license. How would I get to school? I wasn't organized enough at 15 to pay the rent, manage my schedule, go on auditions, work and take care of my basic needs," she said.

Some children don't have a choice. In 2012, 30,000 children emancipated from their foster care homes, a number that is increasing. Lemley says those children face higher rates of incarceration, homelessness, and mental illness.

Still, Lemley says she still receives calls from kids seeking a legal recourse to get out of their foster care homes. Her answer is simple.

"Our guidance is that you need your foster care placement changed," she says, "The answer is not to go at it alone."

> *"In his mind, it was reasonable to ask that I emancipate myself and work for a living."*

My Father Offered Me Emancipation, but I Refused It

Personal Narrative

Alyssa Bereznak

In the following viewpoint, Alyssa Bereznak contends that her father's request that she emancipate herself was rooted in the philosophy of objectivism. Bereznak claims that the objectivism of Ayn Rand is a philosophy focused on obsession with the individual and on pursuing one's own self-interest. Bereznak asserts that this was at the root of her father's request that she emancipate and become self-sufficient—a request that she turned down during her sophomore year in high school. Bereznak is a technology columnist at Yahoo.

My parents split up when I was 4. My father, a lawyer, wrote the divorce papers himself and included one specific rule: My mother was forbidden to raise my brother and me religiously. She agreed, dissolving Sunday church and Bible study with one

Alyssa Bereznak, "How Ayn Rand Ruined My Childhood," *Salon*, April 5, 2011. This article first appeared in Salon.com, at http://www.Salon.com. An online version remains in the Salon archives. Reprinted with permission.

swift signature. Mom didn't mind; she was agnostic and knew we didn't need religion to be good people. But a disdain for faith wasn't the only reason he wrote God out of my childhood. There was simply no room in our household for both Jesus Christ and my father's one true love: Ayn Rand.

You might be familiar with Rand from a high school reading assignment. Perhaps a Tea Partyer acquaintance name-dropped her in a debate on individual rights. Or maybe you've heard the film adaptation of her magnum opus *Atlas Shrugged* is due out April 15 [2011]. In short, she is a Russian-born American novelist who championed her self-taught philosophy of objectivism through her many works of fiction. Conservatives are known to praise her for her support of laissez-faire economics and meritocracy. Liberals tend to criticize her for being too simplistic. I know her more intimately as the woman whose philosophy dictates my father's every decision.

Ayn Rand's Objectivism

What is objectivism? If you'd asked me that question as a child, I could have trotted to the foyer of my father's home and referenced a framed quote by Rand that hung there like a cross. It read: "My philosophy, in essence, is the concept of man as a heroic being, with his own happiness as the moral purpose of his life, with productive achievement as his noblest activity, and reason as his only absolute." As a little kid I interpreted this to mean: Love yourself. Nowadays, Rand's bit is best summed up by the rapper Drake, who sang: "Imma do me."

Dad wasn't always a Rand zealot. He was raised in a Catholic family and went to church every week. After he and my mother got married in 1982, they shopped around for a church. He was looking for something to live by, but he couldn't find it in traditional organized religion.

Then he discovered objectivism. I don't know exactly why he sparked to Rand. He claimed the philosophy appealed to him because it's based solely on logic. It also conveniently quenched his lawyer's thirst to always be right. It's not uncommon for people to seek out belief systems, whether political or spiritual, that make them feel good about how they already live their lives. Ultimately, I suspect Dad was drawn to objectivism because, unlike so many altruistic faiths, it made him feel good about being selfish.

Needless to say, Dad's newfound obsession with the individual didn't pan out so well with the woman he married. He was always controlling, but he became even more so. In the end, my mother moved out, but objectivism stayed. My brother and I switched off living at each parent's house once a week.

It was odd growing up, at least part-time, in an objectivist house. My father reserved long weekends to attend Ayn Rand Institute conferences held in Orange County, California. He would return with a tan and a pile of new reading material for my brother and me. While other kids my age were going to Bible study, I took evening classes from the institute via phone. (I half-listened while clicking through lolcat photos.)

Objectivism and Self-Interest
Our objectivist education, however, was not confined to lectures and books. One time, at dinner, I complained that my brother was hogging all the food.

"He's being selfish!" I whined to my father.

"Being selfish is a good thing," he said. "To be selfless is to deny one's self. To be selfish is to embrace the self, and accept your wants and needs."

It was my dad's classic response—a grandiose philosophical answer to a simple real-world problem. But who cared about logic? All I wanted was another serving of mashed potatoes.

Still, Rand's philosophy was well-suited for the self-absorbed tween I was becoming. Her books were packed with riveting plot twists and sexy architects—easy reading as long as you skimmed over the occasional four-page, didactic rant. Around the time I began exploring Rand's literature, my parents began an epic legal battle over child support. I felt isolated by the conflict and found solace in Rand's message: You must rely on yourself for happiness.

Just as many use faith as a reason to continue during hard times, objectivism helped me stay strong throughout my parents' legal battle. I got a part-time job, played field hockey, ran for student government and joined the yearbook staff. I argued with a Birkenstock-clad substitute teacher the day he showed Michael Moore's classic underdog-bites-back documentary *Roger and Me* in government class. He looked at me in disbelief as I, a skinny blond girl with braces, insisted that General Motors CEO [chief executive officer] Roger Smith had every right to ruin the lives of Flint, Mich., citizens. On weekends I argued with my friends that global warming didn't exist. I hoarded my accomplishments at school, convinced I'd earned them all on my own. Meanwhile, my mother quietly packed my lunch every day.

Soon, however, I began to question whether my father's philosophical beliefs were simply a justification of his own needs. As soon as the legal drama erupted, he refused to pay for even the smallest things, declaring, "Your mother is suing me," in defensive sound bites, as though it explained everything.

Can I buy new shoes? A couple bucks for the movies? *Your mother is suing me.*

Twenty dollars for a class field trip? *Your mother is suing me.*

From what I understood of his favorite capitalist champion, any form of altruism was evil. But how could that kind of blanket self-interest extend to his own children, the people he was legally and morally bound to take care of? What was I supposed to do, fend for myself?

A Request for Emancipation

The answer to my question came on an autumn weekend during my sophomore year in high school. I was hosting a Harry Potter-themed float party in our driveway, a normal ritual to prepare decorations for my high school quad the week of homecoming.

As I was painting a cardboard owl, my father asked me to come inside the house. He and his new wife sat me down at the dinner table with grave faces.

"We were wondering if you would petition to be emancipated," he said in his lawyer voice.

"What does that mean?" I asked, picking at the mauve paint on my hands. I later discovered that for most kids, declaring emancipation is an extreme measure—something you do if your parents are crack addicts or deadbeats.

"You would need to become financially independent," he said. "You could work for me at my law firm and pay rent to live here."

This was my moment of truth as an objectivist. If I believed in the glory of the individual, I would've signed the petition papers then and there. But as much as Rand's novels had taught me to believe in meritocracy, they had not prepared me to go it alone financially and emotionally. I began to cry and refused.

Hardcore objectivists often criticize liberals for basing decisions on emotion, rather than reason. My father saw our family politics no differently. In his mind, it was reasonable to ask that I emancipate myself and work for a living. To me, it felt like he was asking me to sacrifice my childhood so he didn't have to pay child support. To me, it felt like abandonment.

Nearly a year after that conversation, my parents' legal battle came to an end. In Santa Clara County's record room, the typical family law case occupies the space of a small manila folder. My parents' case filled several shelves. A judge decided my father would have to pay my mother both what he owed in child support and her attorney fees—an amount that totaled about $120,000.

Dad's only choice was to sell our house. I moved to Mom's and saw him for the occasional restaurant lunch or family holiday. The distance between us grew wider when I went off to college. He'd call me every other month to play 20-minute catch-up before he had to rush back to work. More consistent, however, were his e-mails. Forwarded from the daily objectivist newsletter he subscribed to, each one had a title like "George W. Bush, Genius" or "Obama the Pathetic." They continue to pile up in my inbox, mostly unread. Every once in a while, I'll click on one, hoping to find a "How are you?" or "What's new?" to no avail. It's a hopeless exercise. I learned long ago that an objectivist like my father simply doesn't care to know.

> *"The 20,000 youth who age out of the foster care system annually need public support to assist them to become healthy, productive, and contributing members of society."*

The Emancipation of Foster Care Youth Is Far from Ideal

Alfreda P. Iglehart and Rosina M. Becerra

In the following viewpoint, Alfreda P. Iglehart and Rosina M. Becerra argue that foster care youth often age out of the system, becoming emancipated at age eighteen, without the necessary supports to avoid a variety of negative outcomes. The authors contend that public policies need to address the poor health and employment outcomes of these youth who come of age within the foster care system. Iglehart is Associate Professor of Social Welfare at the University of California, Los Angeles's Luskin School of Public Affairs and Becerra is a professor and Director of Field Education at the Luskin School of Public Affairs.

*F*oster care emancipation describes the process by which a youth in foster care is "freed" from or "ages out" of the public child welfare system. The term *aging out of foster care* is beginning to replace *emancipation* because it is becoming increasingly clear that there is very little "freedom" associated

Alfreda P. Iglehart and Rosina M. Becerra, "Foster Care Emancipation," *Encyclopedia of Family Health*, Martha Craft-Rosenberg and Shelley-Rae Pehler, eds. Thousand Oaks, CA: SAGE Reference, 2011, pp. 512–514. Reproduced by permission.

President Bill Clinton signs the Foster Care Independence Act in 1999, providing states with more funding for foster care programs. Foster care youth often age out of the system and face a variety of negative health and employment outcomes. © AP Photo/Greg Gibson.

with leaving the foster care system. Reaching the age of adulthood means that the young person is no longer eligible for financial support by the governmental institutions that are responsible for the safety and care of dependent and neglected children. In the United States and most Western countries, this age is 18 years.

Youth in Foster Care

When parents are not able to care for a child because of substance abuse, mental illness, incarceration, and myriad other reasons resulting in parental neglect, the public child welfare system may remove that child from the home. In addition, a child who is experiencing emotional, physical, or sexual abuse may also be removed from the home. That child may be placed in foster care with another family who will foster (care for and look after) him or her until reunification with the family of origin can be achieved. If family reunification does not take place, the child may remain in foster care until he or she reaches the legal age of adulthood (age of emancipation).

If a young person is likely to remain in a foster home from the age of 16 years until the age of 18 years, then he or she is known today as a transitional aged youth. This transition can be abrupt and these youth often find themselves without a home, a job, or their family. This transition to adulthood is fraught with enormous challenges that are not typically experienced by the vast majority of non-foster youth. These youth who age out of care are at a significantly higher risk for homelessness, unemployment, educational deficits, unplanned pregnancies, welfare dependency, and health and mental health problems. This entry discusses some of these concerns as well as the disproportionate representation of minority youth, particularly African American youth, in the foster care system.

Some of these emerging adults reconnect with their families of origin only to find that many of the problems that required removal from their homes and foster care placement still remain. In these situations, there is little institutional response to, or support for, their plight. Many of these young adults are disproportionately faced with the need for additional social services and supports after they have endured placement instability (multiple foster care placements).

Negative Outcomes of Foster Care

Placement instability is also associated with poor health and mental health outcomes. Physical examinations might not occur as needed, and chronic health problems may not be properly monitored. A change in placement can also result in needed medication not following the youth to the next foster home. Separation from family, for whatever reason, may lead to anxiety and depression. Multiple placements can dampen a youth's ability and desire to forge close, trusting relationships with adults and peers. This lack of attachment may follow the youth into adulthood.

Foster care instability is associated with educational disruption (changing schools frequently) that adversely affects academic achievement. About 50% of foster youth complete high school before they leave foster care. Many go on to complete a general equivalency diploma (GED) at a later date. Although a GED is better than no high school certificate, there are differences in the career pathways available to high school diploma completers versus the GED completers. A very small proportion of emancipating youth enter postsecondary education and of those who do, the completion rate is very low, about 10%. Consequently, most emancipating youth have a limited career trajectory and face a future with fewer resources for housing, food, and medical care, especially in a world in which some postsecondary education is needed.

Former foster youth, like most vulnerable youth, are at risk for unemployment or minimum wage employment because of the few marketable skills they possess. Clearly, their prospects are dimmed because of limited education or vocational training. Another factor is the lack of support and encouragement former foster youth receive from family and kin networks. The Independent Living Programs (ILPs) are designed to prepare youth (while they are in foster care) for life after aging out of foster care. Studies show that many of these ILPs have limited utility for these youth because the programs often fail to provide hands-on experiences and may occur well in advance of emancipation. Because the programs are voluntary, youth may decide not to participate in them or think they do not need them.

Risks for Emancipating Foster Care Youth

According to public policy, emancipating youth should leave the foster care system with a high school diploma, documentation such as a birth certificate and social security number, and enrollment in Medicaid, for which they are eligible until the age of 21. However, numerous young people leave foster care with none or

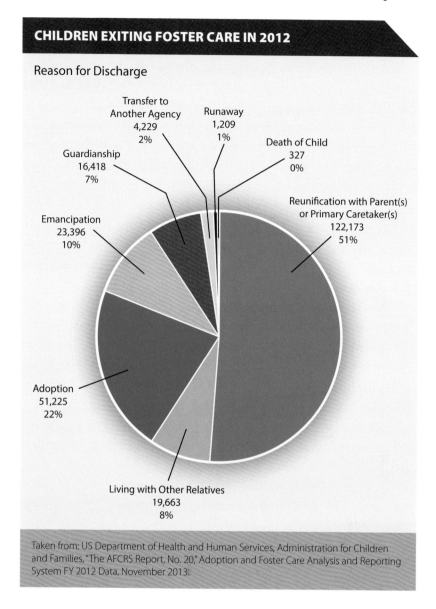

CHILDREN EXITING FOSTER CARE IN 2012

Reason for Discharge

Transfer to
Another Agency
4,229
2%

Runaway
1,209
1%

Death of Child
327
0%

Guardianship
16,418
7%

Reunification with Parent(s)
or Primary Caretaker(s)
122,173
51%

Emancipation
23,396
10%

Adoption
51,225
22%

Living with Other Relatives
19,663
8%

Taken from: US Department of Health and Human Services, Administration for Children and Families, "The AFCRS Report, No. 20," Adoption and Foster Care Analysis and Reporting System FY 2012 Data, November 2013.

only one or two of these documents. Those youth without a birth certificate are unable to obtain a social security card, enroll in various educational programs, apply for driver's license, or prove who they are.

These former foster care youth are more likely than their non-foster care peers to be involved in risky behaviors such as unprotected sexual encounters, drug and alcohol abuse, and criminal activities. They have higher rates of health issues such as HIV/AIDS, unplanned pregnancies, sexually transmitted diseases, and other infectious diseases. They leave the child welfare system with little knowledge of how to access or navigate the health care system. Their health care needs are often greater than their peers, but they do not have the resources to pay for treatment and they do not have the knowledge of how to access services. Because a high percentage of these youth lack health insurance and are unaware of their eligibility for Medicaid or any other resources, any health or mental health condition is likely to receive delayed or no treatment.

It is estimated that as high as 70% of youth transitioning out of the foster care system suffer from one or more mental health problems severe enough to justify mental health care. The most common disorders are depression, anxiety disorders, substance abuse, and post-traumatic stress disorder. When these disorders go untreated, they often result in disruptive or criminal behavior that places these young people at risk for incarceration. Some researchers estimate that 50% of all individuals who are incarcerated are former foster care youth.

There are approximately 500,000 children across the United States who are currently in the foster care system. Of this group, about 20,000 age out of care annually and are expected to transition to adult independence. African American and Hispanic children are disproportionately represented in the child welfare system. It is estimated that 30% of foster children are African American, even though African American children represent about 15% of all children under the age of 18 years in the country. In some states, this is similarly true for Hispanic and American Indian children. Children of color represent nearly half of all children in the foster care system. Additionally, virtually all the children in the system are from poor or low-income families.

Overall, public child welfare is a system for poor and nonwhite children. For these reasons, it is critical that young people age out of foster care equipped with the skills, knowledge, and resources necessary for self-sufficiency.

Government Policies Regarding Foster Care

Although Title IV-E of the Social Security Act added the ILPs to address the needs of emancipating youth, the majority of public policy efforts were aimed at youth in foster care, and little attention was directed toward the aging out process. Policymakers recognized that former foster youth in general were not realizing a healthy and productive life compared to their same-aged peers. In 1999 Congress passed the Foster Care Independence Act (FCIA) to replace Title IV-E. This act provided the states with a dedicated funding stream for programs for foster youth and increased funds for ILPs. The act established the John H. Chafee Foster Care Independent Living Program, commonly referred to as the Chafee Act. This act provides flexible funding to states to develop and implement independent living services to all foster care children who are expected to remain in care until the age of 18 years. It allows Medicare coverage, as well as room and board, for former foster youth until the age of 21. These provisions are to be carried out by the states so they can tailor the programs to meet the needs of their foster youth population. The implementation of state programs designed to help emancipated youth are uneven in their effectiveness. In 2001, the FCIA was amended to include the Promoting Safe and Stable Families Act to help states pay postsecondary education and training and related costs as one means to support those former foster youth to attend college if they were academically able.

The states may also access other programs, such as Temporary Assistance for Needy Families, the Workforce Investment Act, and Medicaid. Although these programs do not specifically target youth transitioning out of foster care, they meet other eligibility requirements such as unemployment, homelessness, and single parenthood. These youth are also eligible for programs in other systems such as the mental health system. However, this situation still leaves the youth to try to navigate various systems and unconnected services by themselves.

The Fostering Connections to Success and Increasing Adoptions Act of 2008 (H.R. 6893) recognizes that former foster youth might not be ready for independent living at the age of 18 years. This act permits states to extend foster care supports and services, under certain conditions, up to the age of 21. Thus, leaving the foster care system becomes an option for the young person rather than a policy requirement. State child welfare and state Medicaid agencies are expected to work together to forge a plan to improve the mental and physical health outcomes of this population. This option provides additional time for ensuring the youth learn the life skills needed to support a successful transition to adulthood. Extending Medicaid and other entitlements to youth beyond this age of 18 years is now open to states, and many are moving in this direction. This flexibility in policy can provide the safety net that these youth need to move more incrementally into adulthood. The 20,000 youth who age out of the foster care system annually need public support to assist them to become healthy, productive, and contributing members of society.

| "*The scariest part about being in foster care for me was turning 18.*"

I Aged Out of the Foster Care System and Became Homeless

Personal Narrative

LaTasha C. Watts

In the following viewpoint, LaTasha C. Watts recounts her experience being emancipated to adulthood within the foster care system. She contends that there was little support when she turned eighteen years of age and that she and many others suffer when they leave foster care. Watts is founder and executive director of The Purple Project, a support and resource network for foster children who have "aged out" of the foster care system, and author of I'm Not Broken Just A Little Twisted: Scenes Through the Mind of a Foster Child.

Most people wake up each day with a mom, a dad or some form of a family structure. However, the youth in foster care who have this type of life are few and far between. I entered foster care as an infant, and my childhood would forever remain "chained" there. Growing up in care was very difficult for me. I had no sense of self worth or identity and most of the time I felt alone, even though I had a foster family. I barely remember—important parts of my life, like a year that I excelled in track or my drama performances, because no one was there to support me or cheer me on.

Aging Out of Foster Care

I was never adopted, and I grew up feeling that no one ever really wanted or loved me. As a result I spent my entire childhood and the majority of my adult life drifting in and out of relationships, and struggling to grasp the concepts of life, love, trust and, most of all, family. The scariest part about being in foster care for me was turning 18. The average kid cannot wait to turn eighteen, graduate from high school and get ready for their journey to college or to travel down that brave road to adulthood. However, by the time I turned 18, the road to college was a distant memory.

Instead I was constantly looking for a place to live, couch surfing, trying to figure out how to pay for my most basic needs—on some days I even had to figure out how I was going to eat (and believe you me, there were plenty of nights that I went to bed hungry). This is the one area where I feel the foster care system, as a whole, has dropped the ball.

"Aging out," is what they call it, and it affects thousands of kids across our nation; unlike the "Harlem shake" or some gaudy fashion, this "trend" never gets a million hits on YouTube, and you can't pick it up and read about it in the latest fashion magazine. What you can do is see homeless teens skateboarding till nightfall, or hanging out in a library or local mall to keep themselves busy, to avoid thinking about the hunger in their bellies or the agonizing reality that they have no place to sleep.

The Reality of the End of Foster Care

This is what the end of foster care meant for me, and thousands of foster kids across this country. Not *The Blind Side* fairy tale ending you thought it would be, huh? Sure, that movie was based on a true story, but for thousands of us there is no Sandra Bullock—or her real-life equivalent—to whisk us away in a fancy car to a better life. Look at it this way . . . children are being removed daily from unimaginable situations of abuse and neglect; anywhere from physical abuse to the lack of proper food, housing, and unsanitary conditions. Those kids are removed from their families and now placed in the foster care system—understandably so. But many of them are well cared for, only to age out into the same conditions that originally landed them in foster care. This, without a doubt, needs to change!

In all fairness, there are some amazing foster care endings, where youth have thrived and they have done very well after exiting foster care. However wouldn't you want every child to leave foster care with a success story?

> "It has long been recognized in this state
> that for certain purposes, emancipation
> of minors may occur even in the
> absence of a statute."

A Married, Independent Minor Can Be Considered Legally Emancipated

The Washington State Supreme Court's Decision

Lloyd W. Shorett

In the following viewpoint, Lloyd W. Shorett, writing for the Supreme Court of Washington, argues that a minor may be considered emancipated for the purpose of consenting to surgery. Shorett contends that a married eighteen-year-old who had not yet reached the age of majority (twenty-one years at the time) could be considered mature enough to be emancipated for medical purposes because he had his own family, made his own living, and maintained his own home. Shorett was a Superior Court judge and served temporarily as a justice on the Supreme Court of Washington.

This litigation results from a vasectomy operation performed upon the person of Albert G. Smith, the appellant, by the re-

Lloyd W. Shorett, Majority opinion, *Smith v. Seibly*, Supreme Court of Washington, August 31, 1967.

spondent, Walter W. Seibly, a practicing physician at Clarkston. At the time of the operation the appellant was 18 years old, married and the father of a child. He was gainfully employed, supported his family and maintained a home for himself, his wife and child. He was afflicted with a progressive muscular disease, myasthenia gravis, which is chronic and incurable and would possibly affect his future earning capacity and ability to support his family. Under these circumstances he and his wife decided to limit their family by having appellant sterilized.

The Vasectomy of a Minor

The family doctor refused to perform the operation because of appellant's youth and the doctor's knowledge of the instability of the marriage. Whereupon, appellant and his wife sought another doctor and on March 9, 1961, visited the respondent's offices requesting that respondent perform the vasectomy. The appellant represented that the sterilization was desired because of his affliction with myasthenia gravis. Respondent illustrated the operation with a diagram and explained that it would result in permanent sterilization. There is a dispute as to whether the appellant represented that he was of legal age [the age of majority in Washington at the time was 21]. The respondent read aloud and presented the following statement to appellant and his wife:

> TO WHOM IT MAY CONCERN: We, the undersigned, hereby consent to the sterilization operation to be performed on the husband, having been told that the operation is a permanent thing, that there is no chance for a reestablishment of a viable sperm in the semen.

The doctor then told appellant and his wife to go home, think about the operation and if they still wished it performed, sign the paper and return to his office.

Twelve days later appellant returned, presented the consent signed by himself and his wife, and the operation was performed.

After appellant reached his majority [21 years old], he brought this action alleging that the respondent was negligent in performing the vasectomy upon an infant of 18 years, was negligent in failing to explain to appellant the permanent consequences of the surgery, and that such surgery was performed without valid permission. The appellant asked damages in the amount of $52,000. The respondent's answer denied the allegations of negligence and liability and alleged that the appellant was barred from recovery because he had signed a consent to the operation.

Although the complaint contained allegations based on a theory of negligence, all parties agree that the trial court properly submitted the case to the jury on an assault theory. One of the instructions read: ". . . The vasectomy is an assault and battery if surgery was performed without valid consent." Appellant's theory was that a minor could not give valid consent to such surgery. The respondent's view, adopted by the trial court, was that under some conditions a minor may be emancipated for the purpose of giving consent to surgery. The jury returned a verdict for respondent and judgment having been entered thereon, this appeal followed. . . .

The Emancipation of Minors

Appellant . . . contends that error was committed in giving instructions Nos. 13, 14, 15 and 16 and in refusing to give appellant's requested instructions Nos. 7 and 8.

The exceptions taken to the trial court's action on these instructions were all on one ground, namely, that appellant, being a minor, could not give consent to the operation, that his consent was void, and that parental consent was necessary to insulate respondent from liability. It has long been recognized in this state that for certain purposes, emancipation of minors may occur even in the absence of a statute.

Respondent contends that appellant was emancipated for the purpose of giving consent to the operation, or, at least that a jury

Proposed Jury Instructions in
Smith v. Seibly

Proposed Instruction No. 7:

"You are instructed that under the law of the State of Washington, a male less than 21 years old is an infant.

"You are further instructed that no operation may be performed by a surgeon upon an infant unless consent is first obtained of the natural guardian or parents of the infant, unless the operation is for the benefit of the infant and is done with the purpose of saving his life or limb.

"Therefore, if you find from the evidence in this case that the defendant Walter Seibly performed a surgical operation upon the plaintiff at a time when the plaintiff was less than 21 years old, and if you further find that at the time of said operation the defendant Walter Seibly had not obtained the consent of the parents of the plaintiff, then you should completely disregard any evidence of a release having been signed by the plaintiff.

"This is the law, even though you should find that the plaintiff was married at the time the operation was performed."

Proposed Instruction No. 8:

"You are instructed that in this case the Court has determined as a matter of law that the operation performed by the defendant Seibly on the plaintiff was an unauthorized operation.

"You are therefore directed to return a verdict in favor of the plaintiff and against the defendants Seibly, and fix damages in accordance with the instructions the Court has given you concerning damages."

Smith v. Seibly, *Supreme Court of Washington,*
August 31, 1967.

question was presented on this issue. In *American Prods. Co. v. Villwock* (1941), this court quoted from 1 Schouler, Domestic Relations (6th ed.) 897, § 807 as follows:

> "Emancipation" of a child is the relinquishment by the parent of control and authority over the child, conferring on him the right to his earnings and terminating the parent's legal duty to support the child. It may be express, as by voluntary agreement of parent and child, or implied from such acts and conduct as import consent; it may be conditional or absolute, complete or partial.

To the same effect see *DeLay v. DeLay* (1959). The subject "What amounts to implied emancipation of a minor child" is annotated in 165 A.L.R. 723, 745, where it is stated:

> [I]t is settled by the weight of authority that the marriage of a minor with parent's consent (according to some cases) or even without the parent's consent (according to other cases) works an emancipation, for the reason that the marriage gives rise to a new relation inconsistent with the subjection to the control and care of the parent. In such case the emancipated child is the head of a new family and as such is subject to obligations and duties to his wife and children which require him to be the master of himself, his time, his labor, earnings, and conduct.

We limit this discussion of the instructions to the exception taken by appellant.

The Ability to Consent to Surgery

Tested by the exception taken, the instructions given were not erroneous. A married minor, 18 years of age, who has successfully completed high school and is the head of his own family, who earns his own living and maintains his own home, is emancipated for the purpose of giving a valid consent to surgery if a full disclosure of the ramifications, implications and probable consequences of the surgery has been made by the doctor in

A couple meets with a health care professional. The Supreme Court of Washington decision of Smith v. Seibly *(1967) gave independent married minors the right to make medical choices.* © iStock.com/webphotographeer.

terms which are fully comprehensible to the minor. Thus, age, intelligence, maturity, training, experience, economic independence or lack thereof, general conduct as an adult and freedom from the control of parents are all factors to be considered in such a case.

Appellant was married, independent of parental control and financial support and it was for the jury to decide if he was sufficiently intelligent, educated and knowledgeable to make a legally binding decision. As we stated in *Grannum v. Berard* (1967): "The mental capacity necessary to consent to a surgical operation is a question of fact to be determined from the circumstances of each individual case."

The jury was correctly instructed as to the factors to be weighed in determining appellant's capacity to consent to the operation.

> "Whether a minor has the capacity to
> consent to medical treatment depends
> upon the age, ability, experience,
> education, training, and degree of
> maturity or judgment obtained by
> the minor."

There Is a Mature Minor Exception to Parental Consent in Medical Decisions

The Tennessee Supreme Court's Decision

Frank Drowota

In the following viewpoint Frank Drowota, writing for the Supreme Court of Tennessee, determines that there exists a mature minor exception to the common law doctrine that parents should be required to consent to medical treatment of their children. Drowota contends that there exists a so-called Rule of Sevens, whereby minors between the ages of fourteen and twenty-one are presumed to have the capacity to make major decisions, including decisions about health care. Drowota claims that in the Cardwell v. Bechtol *case there is evidence of informed consent and maturity consistent with allowing a mature minor exception. Drowota is a former chief justice of the Tennessee Supreme Court.*

Frank Drowota, Majority opinion, *Cardwell v. Bechtol*, Supreme Court of Tennessee, February 9, 1987.

An issue of first impression in Tennessee is raised in this appeal as to whether Tennessee should adopt a mature minor exception to the common law rule that requires a physician to obtain parental consent before treating a minor. This case arose out of treatment administered by Defendant, Dr. E.L Bechtol, to Sandra K. Cardwell, the daughter of Robert and Wilma Cardwell. Defendant is a doctor of osteopathy. At the time of treatment, Sandra Cardwell was a minor. The suit was instituted by the Plaintiffs, Sandra Cardwell, individually, and by her parents, both individually and as next friends on behalf of their daughter.

A Minor's Back Condition

While Sandra Cardwell (Ms. Cardwell) was attending high school, she had suffered from persistent but intermittent back pain. She first saw her family physician in the summer of 1981 for this problem. Subsequently, in early October, 1981, she went to the Knoxville Orthopedic Clinic where she was seen by Dr. Stevens. His preliminary diagnosis was that she was displaying symptoms associated with a herniated disc; he recommended that she be hospitalized for further tests and therapy. Her parents decided to obtain a second opinion before acceding to hospitalization and she went to see Dr. McMahon, an orthopedic specialist, in Oak Ridge on October 15, 1981; he concurred in the diagnosis and recommendation of Dr. Stevens.

On November 9, 1981, she was hospitalized at St. Mary's Medical Center in Knoxville. She was attended by Doctors Stevens and Wallace and underwent conservative treatment consisting primarily of physical therapy and injections. A recommended myelogram was rejected by her parents. A conservative course of treatment was continued following her discharge from the hospital on November 16, 1981. Dr. Sidney Wallace assumed treatment of Ms. Cardwell; he saw her several more times during the remainder of 1981 and in the early months of 1982. Apparently, both Ms. Cardwell and her parents hoped to avoid any necessity to resort to surgery.

Although her condition did not bother her continuously and she was usually able to participate in her normal high school activities, she was not obtaining any significant relief for her pain, despite the therapy and treatment she received under Dr. Wallace's care. In March, 1982, Dr. Wallace again recommended pre-surgical, diagnostic testing to identify definitely the nature of the problem, but Ms. Cardwell and her parents evidently continued to resist consideration of surgery. On April 26, 1982, having taken her mother's car to school, Ms. Cardwell left school early and went to see the family physician for treatment of a sore throat. With her mother's permission, she went to the family doctor's office alone. After her appointment with this doctor, she spontaneously decided that she would go to see Defendant, an osteopath who had treated her father's back condition on several occasions in the past. She had not told her parents that she was going to see Defendant but decided to do so on this day because her back was hurting her.

A Complaint of Battery

Defendant is a licensed osteopath but because he has been blind for most of his life, he limits his practice to manipulative treatments to adjust or realign the skeletal system. He conducts his sole practice with the assistance of his wife and daughter, who maintain his records. He was alone in his office when Ms. Cardwell came to see him. She told Defendant her name and that her father had been one of his patients; she also informed him of her symptoms and of the diagnoses of the orthepedic specialists she had seen. Defendant concluded, after examining her briefly, that a herniated disc was not her problem and treated her with manipulations involving her neck, spine, and legs for subluxation of the spine and bilateral sacroiliac slip. The treatment lasted for about 15 minutes, after which he asked her to return several times during the next few weeks for further manipulations. Ms. Cardwell wrote her name, age, and address down on a card Defendant supplied for this purpose and then paid his fee of

$25.00 with one of her father's blank, signed checks, which had been given to her to be used when she needed money.

After Ms. Cardwell left Defendant's office, she began to experience a tingling and numbing sensation in her legs. She drove to her aunt's house and lay down to take a nap. She was awakened by severe pain about an hour later. The pain was such that she had difficulty walking, but having driven her mother's car, she was obligated to pick her up from work. She found she had difficulty driving and when she reached her mother's place of employment, her pain had become very intense. By the time she and her mother arrived at home, she was no longer able to walk by herself. Later in the evening, she was driven to the emergency room at St. Mary's Medical Center in Knoxville and was subsequently admitted. Over the course of the evening, she also developed urinary retention problems and had to be catheterized.

During the next few days, she underwent diagnostic testing, which confirmed that she had a herniated disc, and a laminectomy was performed on April 29, 1982. Although no visible nerve damage was apparent, she continued to experience bladder and bowel retention and had continued difficulty walking as well as decreased sensation in her legs and buttocks. Her condition has improved gradually since her surgery, but she had not yet regained normal bowel control or complete sensation in her buttocks and one of her legs at the time of trial.

This action was filed on April 22, 1983, in Anderson County Circuit Court. The initial complaint alleged only medical malpractice (in the diagnosis and treatment of Ms. Cardwell's condition) but the complaint was subsequently amended to include counts of battery (failure to obtain parental consent), negligent failure to obtain consent, and failure to obtain informed consent. . . .

A Lack of Parental Consent

On April 26, 1982, the date of Ms. Cardwell's treatment by Defendant, she was 17 years, 7 months of age, a senior in high

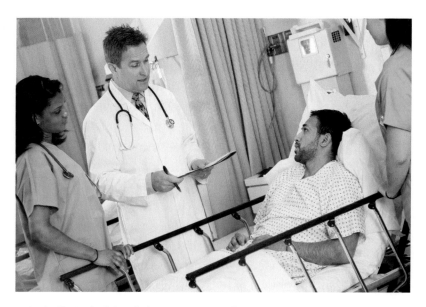

In Cardwell v. Bechtol *(1987), the Supreme Court of Tennessee recognized that minors achieve varying degrees of maturity and responsibility. The court ruled that minors over the age of fourteen are presumed to have the capacity to make major health-care decisions.* © iStock. com/asiseeit.

school with good grades, and was planning to attend college. She had been licensed to drive since she was 16 years old. As a routine practice from the time she was 14 years old, she had permission to use her father's checking account; she carried several signed, blank checks in lieu of cash and had been very responsible in the exercise of this privilege. Testimony consistently characterized Ms. Cardwell as a mature young woman who acted somewhat older than her age. Her parents permitted her substantial discretion because of her demonstrated maturity.

On the day she went to see Defendant, she had taken her mother's car so that she could go by herself to see the family physician about a sore throat. She had left school early and with her parents' permission had gone to this doctor's office alone, where she was examined and treated by the family doctor, who had not personally obtained parental consent. She decided to see Defendant on her own initiative because she knew her father had been to see him and she thought that Defendant might be able to provide some relief for her back pain. She had not told her parents that she was going to see Defendant and apparently had not been encouraged to do so by her parents. Although she did not know exactly what manipulative therapy involved, she was generally aware of the kind of practice an osteopath had. She also testified that Defendant did not treat her against her will.

Defendant testified that Ms. Cardwell seemed to him to be a mature young woman. While generally minors are accompanied by adults when they come to him for treatment, and parental consent is ordinarily obtained for treatment, Ms. Cardwell's demeanor led him to think that she was of age and that she had come to him because he had previously treated her father. He did not believe it was necessary to inquire about parental consent in this case. . . .

The Rule of Sevens

Recognition that minors achieve varying degrees of maturity and responsibility (capacity) has been part of the common law for well over a century. The rule of capacity has sometimes been known as the Rule of Sevens: under the age of seven, no capacity; between seven and fourteen, a rebuttable presumption of no capacity; between fourteen and twenty-one, a rebuttable presumption of capacity. In Tennessee and elsewhere, the rule of capacity of minors has been generally applied in criminal cases. The Rule of Sevens has been applied in the context of torts as well. The competency of minors to testify as witnesses has also been measured by the common law Rule of Sevens.

In addition, the Legislature has enacted several statutes that are consistent with or merely codify the Rule of Sevens established at common law. Under T.C.A. § 37-1-134(a), a minor may be tried as an adult in criminal cases if the "child was sixteen (16) years or more of age at the time of the alleged conduct, or the child was more than fourteen (14) years of age if such child was charged with [certain violent crimes]." A minor may obtain a driver's license at 16, but may obtain a learner's permit at age 15 or a special restricted license between the ages of 14 and 16; however a chauffeur's license may not be given to anyone under 18. These statutes clearly recognize the varying degrees of responsibility and maturity of minors 14 years and older.

T.C.A. §§ 1-3-105(1) and 1-3-113(a) now establish the age of majority in this State as 18 years old, except for the purpose of the purchase of alcoholic beverages. That the Legislature has adopted a lower age for attainment of majority indicates persuasively that conditions in society have changed to the extent that maturity is now reached at earlier stages of growth than at the time that the common law recognized the age of majority at 21 years. The conditions and reasons that made 21 the age of majority have been eroded over time. Moreover, the enactment of statutes establishing specific exceptions to the general common law regarding medical treatment of minors also tends to show that the attitudes and customs of society concerning the relative maturity of minors have changed. In any case, these statutory exceptions for medical treatment of minors without parental consent can apply whether the minor is 17 years, eight years, or one year old, although as a practical matter many such statutes will not usually be invoked except in cases of older minors. The mature minor exception, however, is limited by the application of the Rule of Sevens and is an exception to the general rule that parental consent is required to treat minors.

The Mature Minor Exception

Adoption of the mature minor exception to the common law rule is by no means a general license to treat minors without parental consent and its application is dependent on the facts of each case. It must be seen in the context of the tort in question. At this point in the analysis, the issue is whether Ms. Cardwell had the capacity to consent to the treatment administered by Defendant. If Ms. Cardwell had the capacity to consent, then her informed consent would be effective to negate any battery committed by Defendant in the course of his treatment of her. . . .

Whether a minor has the capacity to consent to medical treatment depends upon the age, ability, experience, education, training, and degree of maturity or judgment obtained by the minor, as well as upon the conduct and demeanor of the minor at the time of the incident involved. Moreover, the totality of the circumstances, the nature of the treatment and its risks or probable consequences, and the minor's ability to appreciate the risks and consequences are to be considered. Guided by the presumptions in the Rule of Sevens, these are questions of fact for the jury to decide.

In our opinion, adoption of the mature minor exception to the general common law rule at issue would be wholly consistent with the existing statutory and tort law in this State as part of "the normal course of the growth and development of the law" [*Powell v. Hartford Accident and Indemnity Co.* (1965)]. Accordingly, we hold that the mature minor exception is part of the common law of Tennessee. Its application is a question of fact for the jury to determine whether the minor has the capacity to consent to and appreciate the nature, the risks, and the consequences of the medical treatment involved. In the circumstances of this case, and based on the evidence presented at trial, we think that the jury was justified in concluding that Ms. Cardwell had the ability, maturity, experience, education and judgment at her 17 years, 7 months of age to consent knowingly to medical treatment. "In this case, therefore, the reason for the common law rule does not exist. Where the reason fails the rule should not apply" [*Brown v. Selby* (1960)].

We do not, however, alter the general rule requiring parental consent for the medical treatment of minors. We observe here that under the Rule of Sevens, it would rarely, if ever, be reasonable, absent an applicable statutory exception, for a physician to treat a minor under seven years, and that between the ages of seven and fourteen, the rebuttable presumption is that a minor would not have the capacity to consent; moreover, while between the ages of fourteen and eighteen, a presumption of capacity does arise, that presumption may be rebutted by evidence of incapacity, thereby exposing a physician or care provider to an action for battery.

The Issue of Informed Consent

A complete analysis of the issue of the effectiveness of consent cannot be made without considering whether Ms. Cardwell had sufficient information concerning the risks and consequences of the treatment administered, regardless of her capacity to give actual consent under the mature minor exception. Whether the information she had was sufficient depends on the nature of the treatment, the extent of the risks involved, and the standard of care of the treating physician. . . .

Ms. Cardwell testified that she was not fully cognizant of the nature of spinal manipulative therapy, that she had never undergone such treatment, and that she had never discussed it in any detail with anyone, including Defendant, as of April 26, 1982. She did have a general idea of what the practice of an osteopath involved, considering it similar to that of a chiropractor. She knew that manipulations were involved and that this treatment was the reason she decided to see Defendant. She stated that Defendant did not discuss the nature of the treatment or tell her of any risks, although she did seek Defendant's treatment and manifestly consented to the manipulations. She did tell Defendant the diagnoses of the orthopedic specialists who had previously seen her.

Dr. Michael Eisenstadt, a neurologist, testified as an expert for Plaintiffs. He stated that he was familiar with the standard of care required to obtain informed consent and that older children have a greater capacity to comprehend the nature of the treatment. He was of the opinion that the effectiveness of consent depends on the risks involved in the proposed treatment. He admitted, however, that he was not familiar with the standard of care for an osteopath in informing a patient as to the risks of manipulative treatments.

For Defendant, Dr. James Carson, an osteopath, testified as an expert on the standard of care of osteopaths in informing pa-

The Supreme Court of Appeals of West Virginia's Reasoning

We hold that except in very extreme cases, a physician has no legal right to perform a procedure upon, or administer or withhold treatment from a patient without the patient's consent, nor upon a child without the consent of the child's parents or guardian, unless the child is a mature minor, in which case the child's consent would be required. Whether a child is a mature minor is a question of fact. Whether the child has the capacity to consent depends upon the age, ability, experience, education, training, and degree of maturity or judgment obtained by the child, as well as upon the conduct and demeanor of the child at the time of the procedure or treatment. The factual determination would also involve whether the minor has the capacity to appreciate the nature, risks, and consequences of the medical procedure to be performed, or the treatment to be administered or withheld. Where there is a conflict between the intentions of one or both parents and the minor, the physician's good faith assessment of the minor's maturity level would immunize him or her from liability for the failure to obtain parental consent.

Belcher v. Charleston Area Medical Center,
Supreme Court of Appeals of West Virginia,
1992.

tients of the attendant risks of manipulative treatment and regarding the standard of care in administering such treatment. His opinion was that the effectiveness of consent depends on the treatment and the risks involved. In the case of manipulative treatment, the need to explain is minimal because the treatment is of a minor nature with few risks. He was also of the opinion that the standard of care of osteopaths and medical doctors were not identical. In addition, Defendant testified in his own behalf. He stated that relatively little risk is usually involved in manipulative therapy. He generally did not find it necessary to explain the risks of manipulations unless the patient expressed concern; Ms. Cardwell did not express any apprehension about the treatment at the time he examined and treated her. . . .

The Court's Ruling

Addition of the mature minor exception to the general common law that requires parental consent to treat a minor is consistent with the evolution of the common law of torts in this State and flows as a consequence of those changed conditions that, among other things, have justified the lowering of the age of majority to 18 years of age. We have not found any State policy, legislative or otherwise, that would preclude adoption of the mature minor exception. On the contrary, the statutory law both is generally consistent with the common law on the capacity of minors and supports our conclusion that adoption of this exception undermines no express or apparent legislative policy. Furthermore, this exception is circumscribed by the rebuttable presumptions of the Rule of Sevens and limited by the facts and circumstances of each case; thus, little chance exists that the exception will swallow the rule.

The mature minor exception pretermits the issue of parental consent and we do not address that issue. Ms. Cardwell was only five months short of the age of majority at the time of this incident; the presumption of capacity, therefore, attached under the Rule of Sevens. The jury's verdict, based on instructions incorporating the mature minor exception and the evidence in this case, implicitly found that Ms. Cardwell did have the judgment, ability, education, and training at her 17 years, 7 months to have the capacity to consent and did in fact consent to the Defendant's treatment. The same capacity to consent entails the ability to appreciate and weigh the risks and benefits of the treatment she sought and thus to give informed consent to it. The jury also found that the Defendant complied with the standard of care of his practice in providing her with sufficient information upon which Ms. Cardwell could give informed consent. The treatment was relatively minor, with a minimum risk of injury, and Ms. Cardwell expressed no concern about the treatment at the time it was to be administered. The jury could reasonably have found that Plaintiffs did not show that Defendant had deviated from the standard of care concerning the information ordinarily supplied to obtain informed consent to Defendant's treatment. Consequently, having the capacity to consent and having given informed consent, no battery occurred because Ms. Cardwell's consent was effective on the facts of this case.

> *"A number of 'medical emancipation' statutes allow minors to consent to medical treatment without parental knowledge, approval, or consent."*

Medical Emancipation Statutes Forbid Mandatory Parental Involvement for Student Medical Care

The California Attorney General's Opinion

Bill Lockyer and Susan Duncan Lee

In the following viewpoint, Bill Lockyer and Susan Duncan Lee argue that medical emancipation statutes in California that authorize minors to consent for sensitive medical services preclude school districts from requiring that a student obtain either parental consent prior to receiving confidential medical services or requiring notification of parents if a student leaves school to obtain confidential medical services. Lockyer and Lee contend that requiring parental involvement would destroy the whole concept of certain medical services remaining confidential. Lockyer was attorney general of California from 1999 to 2007 and is currently state treasurer. Lee is the deputy attorney general of California.

Bill Lockyer and Susan Duncan Lee, Opinion no. 04-112, State of California Department of Justice, Office of the Attorney General, November 29, 2004.

The Honorable Dennis Bunting, County Counsel, County of Solano, has requested an opinion on the following questions:

1. May a school district require that a student obtain written parental consent prior to releasing the student from school to receive confidential medical services?

2. May a school district adopt a policy pursuant to which the district will notify a parent when a student leaves school to receive confidential medical services?

Reasons for and Effects of Medical Emancipation

1. A school district may not require that a student obtain written parental consent prior to releasing the student from school to receive confidential medical services.

2. A school district may not adopt a policy pursuant to which the district will notify a parent when a student leaves school to obtain confidential medical services.

Generally speaking, parental consent is required for a minor's medical treatment. There are, however, exceptions, such as when the public interest in preserving the health of a minor takes precedence over the parent's interest in custody and control of the minor. In addition, a number of "medical emancipation" statutes allow minors to consent to medical treatment without parental knowledge, approval, or consent.

Medical emancipation statutes may be separated into two categories. First, they may authorize minors to consent to their own health care treatment because of a particular status. A minor who has become emancipated by reason of a court order, marriage, or active duty in the United States armed forces is considered an adult for purposes of consenting to health care services. In addition, minors who are "self-sufficient" (minors who are 15 or older, living away from home, and managing their own financial affairs regardless of the source of their income) may consent to their own medical care.

Second, they may authorize minors to consent to what are considered to be particularly sensitive medical services. A minor of any age may consent to care related to the prevention or treatment of pregnancy. A minor of age 12 or older may consent to treatment of an infectious, contagious, or communicable disease or to care related to the diagnosis or treatment of rape. A minor of any age may consent to care related to the diagnosis or treatment of sexual assault. A minor of age 12 or older may consent to care related to the diagnosis or treatment of drug-related or alcohol-related problems. A minor of age 12 or older may consent to mental health treatment, counseling, or residential shelter services if (1) the minor is mature enough to participate intelligently, in the opinion of the health care provider, and (2) the minor is either a danger to himself or herself or others without the treatment, or is the alleged victim of incest or child abuse. A minor of any age may consent to HIV testing. Further, the records of these medical services are kept confidential from the minor's parent or guardian, unless the minor consents to such disclosure.

The two questions presented for resolution concern "confidential medical services" provided to school students. For our purposes, such services refer to the second category of medical emancipation statutes—services which, by statute, a minor is authorized to obtain without the consent of or disclosure to a parent or guardian.

The Requirement of Parental Consent

The first question concerns whether a school district may require that a student obtain written parental consent prior to releasing the student from school to receive confidential medical services. We conclude that it may not.

School districts have broad powers to adopt policies in furtherance of their educational purposes, provided they do not act in a manner "in conflict with or inconsistent with, or preempted by, any law." [Education Code.] A policy requiring the prior writ-

The US Supreme Court on Bypass Safeguards

In *Bellotti* [*v. Baird* (1979)] we struck down a statute requiring a minor to obtain the *consent* of both parents before having an abortion, subject to a judicial bypass provision, because the judicial bypass provision was too restrictive, unconstitutionally burdening a minor's right to an abortion. The Court's principal opinion explained that a constitutional parental consent statute must contain a bypass provision that meets four criteria: (i) allow the minor to bypass the consent requirement if she establishes that she is mature enough and well enough informed to make the abortion decision independently; (ii) allow the minor to bypass the consent requirement if she establishes that the abortion would be in her best interests; (iii) ensure the minor's anonymity; and (iv) provide for expeditious bypass procedures.

Lambert v. Wicklund, *US Supreme Court, 1997.*

ten consent of a parent to release a student for confidential medical services would conflict with state law.

The Legislature has established a system of compulsory education for children between the ages of 6 and 18. Attendance at school is excused, however, under specified circumstances. Education Code section 48205, subdivision (a), provides in relevant part:

"Notwithstanding Section 48200 [requiring compulsory full-time education], a pupil shall be excused from school when the absence is: . . .

"(3) For the purpose of having medical, dental, optometrical, or chiropractic services rendered. . . .

"(7) For justifiable personal reasons, including, but not limited to, an appearance in court, attendance at a funeral service, observance of a holiday or ceremony of his or her religion, attendance at religious retreats, or attendance at an employment conference, *when the pupil's absence has been requested in writing by the parent or guardian* and approved by the principal or a designated representative pursuant to uniform standards established by the governing board." (Italics added.)

On its face, subdivision (a)(3) of section 48205 does not require parental consent for an excused medical absence. In contrast is subdivision (a)(7) of the statute, which does require parental consent for certain excused absences. We construe this difference in language as signifying a legislative intent *not* to require parental consent in order to excuse a student for the purpose of obtaining medical services. . . .

We reject the suggestion that Education Code section 46010.1 grants school districts discretion to require parental consent before releasing a student for confidential medical services, notwithstanding the language of Education Code section 48205. Education Code section 46010.1 states:

> "Commencing in the fall of the 1986–87 academic year, the governing board of each school district shall each academic year notify pupils in grades 7–12 inclusive and the parents or guardians of all pupils enrolled in the district, that school authorities may excuse any pupil from the school for the purpose of obtaining confidential medical services without the consent of the pupil's parent or guardian. The notice required pursuant to this section may be included with any other notice given pursuant to this code."

We view this provision as requiring school districts to notify both students and their parents that students are allowed to be excused from school for confidential medical appointments without parental consent.

If a school district *could* require parental consent under the terms of Education Code section 46010.1, the statute would no longer concern "confidential medical services." By definition, such services are kept confidential from the parent or guardian of the pupil. The legislative history of the statute makes clear that the Legislature intended only to ensure that parents of adolescent schoolchildren understand the requirements of the law with respect to medical services that are made "confidential" by statute.

Undermining the Intent of Medical Emancipation Statutes

Most importantly, a school district policy requiring prior written consent of a parent for a student's confidential medical services would undermine the purposes and intent of the medical emancipation statutes. In *American Academy of Pediatrics v. Lungren* [1997], the Supreme Court [of California] observed:

". . . [O]ver the past four decades the Legislature has recognized that, in a variety of specific contexts, the protection of the health of minors may best be served by permitting a minor to obtain medical care without parental consent. These statutes do not reflect a legislative determination that a minor who, for example, has been raped or has contracted a sexually transmitted disease would not benefit from the consultation and advice of a supportive parent. Indeed, as noted, a few of the statutes specifically call upon the treating physician or health care provider to notify and attempt to involve the minor's parents in the treatment process, so long as the circumstances suggest to the health care provider that such involvement will not be detrimental to the health or interests of the minor. Nor do these statutes imply that a minor who, for example, has been sexually assaulted or has a drug or alcohol abuse problem is more mature or knowledgeable than other minors of similar age; a minor who may obtain medical care for such conditions must still obtain parental consent before she or he may obtain, for example, an appendectomy.

"Instead, each of these statutory provisions embodies a legislative recognition that, particularly in matters concerning sexual conduct, minors frequently are reluctant, either because of embarrassment or fear, to inform their parents of

Free HIV testing is given as part of National HIV Testing Day in Atlanta in 2013. Medical emancipation statutes may allow minor students to obtain confidential medical services such as this. © AP Photo/David Goldman.

medical conditions relating to such conduct, and consequently that there is a considerable risk that minors will postpone or avoid seeking needed medical care if they are required to obtain parental consent before receiving medical care for such conditions. To protect their health in these particular circumstances, the statutes authorize minors to receive medical care for these designated conditions without parental consent." . . .

We conclude that a school district may not require that a student obtain written parental consent prior to releasing the student from school to receive confidential medical services.

The Policy of Parental Notification

The second question presented is whether a school district may adopt a policy pursuant to which the district will notify a parent when a student leaves school to obtain confidential medical services. We conclude that such a policy would violate state law.

Notice is not the same as consent, and while the medical emancipation statutes expressly address consent, they do not directly address giving notice. However, we are dealing here with "confidential" medical services. Just like requiring parental consent, a district's notification of a parent regarding a student's absence to receive confidential medical services would destroy the confidentiality of the medical services—contrary to the intent and purposes of the medical emancipating statutes.

Not only may minors seek sensitive medical treatment without parental consent, they have the right to keep the existence of such medical services confidential, even from their parents. These confidentiality statutes evince a clear legislative intent to shield minors, not just from the possibility that parental consent might be withheld for certain medical services, but also from the necessity of revealing that the minor has resorted to those services at all.

Statutes protecting the privacy of medical information are based on the Legislature's awareness that the threat of disclosure might deter persons needing treatment from seeking it. A policy that requires parental notice when a student seeks such services would be inconsistent with the legislative intent to encourage minors to receive medical treatment by protecting the confidentiality of their medical information.

Our conclusion is not inconsistent with the provisions in some of the medical emancipation statutes that require health care professionals to notify the parent or guardian in certain situations. Unlike school officials, health care professionals are qualified to evaluate a minor's capacity to understand his or her treatment options on a case-by-case basis. Furthermore, the statutes give health care professionals the discretion to bypass parental notification when notification would be contrary to the minor patient's welfare. This is the kind of safeguard that has been a consistent feature of the parental consent and notification statutes upheld by the United States Supreme Court. A policy pursuant to which a school would notify a parent whenever a student left school to obtain confidential medical services would afford no such recognized safeguard.

Nor is our conclusion inconsistent with statutes giving parents access to certain information bearing on their children's education, including access to their children's school records. While providing parental access to this information, the Legislature has protected students' rights to informational privacy, specifically regarding confidential medical services and disclosure of personal information to school counselors.

We conclude that a school district may not adopt a policy pursuant to which the school will notify a parent when a student leaves school to receive confidential medical services.

| "There's no clear reason why 18 was chosen for the minimum voting age."

Old Enough to Vote, Old Enough to Smoke?

Jennifer Lai

In the following viewpoint, Jennifer Lai writes that the age of ma-jority, or age when adulthood begins, has been set at age eighteen in most states for arbitrary reasons. Lai contends that this age was chosen because it is the age of voting set by the Twenty-Sixth Amendment. It is unclear why the Twenty-Sixth Amendment specifies eighteen, she contends, but may be because youth usually graduate from high school at eighteen. Lai claims that the different age limit for consumption of alcohol is because young people aged under twenty cause many drunk-driving accidents. Lai is an as-sociate editor at Slate.

New York officials proposed Monday to raise the legal age to buy cigarettes from 18 to 21. In 47 states, the age of majority—the age at which a person has the legal rights and responsibilities of an adult—is 18. Why is 18 considered the age of adulthood?

No Real Reason for Voting at Eighteen

Because that's when people get to vote. Suffrage has long been tied to adulthood and the age of majority in the United States. Before the passage of the 26th Amendment in 1971, 21 was the minimum voting age in most states—and thus served as the age of adulthood in most areas of law. Congress lowered the nationwide voting age to 18 as a response to unrest and passionate debate about the Vietnam War. Many felt that those who were old enough to be drafted into the armed forces should also be able to vote. Retaining a higher age of majority didn't seem to make sense if lawmakers were going to let young people vote at 18, so states began using 18 as the new measure for legal adulthood.

But why 18 for the voting age—and not, say, 16 or 19? It's pretty arbitrary: There's no scientific basis behind the age itself. Although one might assume that most 18-year-olds have reached maturity, researchers have shown that adolescence actually extends into the early 20s. Prior to the 20th century, the age of majority didn't carry much significance: Teenagers were routinely elected to British Parliament, 5-year-olds could sign binding legal contracts to work until the age of 24, and 8-year-olds could be executed for arson.

There's no clear reason why 18 was chosen for the minimum voting age. Some historians point to the development of the education system and the expansion of high school and college enrollments. By the 1960s, attending high school was a near-universal experience among American youth, and most students graduated from high school at age 18. Other cultural shifts in the '60s and '70s changed the way Americans thought of youth, making them seem more adult like. Young people in the Vietnam War era appeared better educated, more politically active, and thus better prepared to take on adult responsibilities than those of previous generations.

© Mike Flannagan/Cartoonstock.com

Preventing Drunk Driving Accidents

So if 18 is the age of adulthood, why is 21 the legal age for consuming alcohol?

Because teenagers were shown to be responsible for a lot of drunk driving accidents. When the 26th Amendment lowered

Mothers Against Drunk Driving (MADD) national president Wendy Hamilton stands in front of a display of people killed by drunk drivers in 2003. Groups such as MADD played a key role in lobbying for the National Minimum Drinking Age Act of 1984. © AP Photo/Bill Haber.

the age of majority, many states experimented in the 1970s with a drinking age below 21. They changed their minds quickly: Accident statistics in those states showed a substantial jump in the number of drunk driving accidents involving 18-to-20-year-olds. Groups like Mothers Against Drunk Driving played a key role in lobbying for the National Minimum Drinking Age Act, which was clearly an anti-drunk-driving measure. When Congress passed the act in 1984, every state was effectively forced to raise its drinking age back to 21.

| "*Whatever the age of majority, it makes absolutely no sense for it to be lower than the drinking age.*"

There Is No Reason to Set the Drinking Age Later than the Age of Majority

Laurence M. Vance

In the following viewpoint, Laurence M. Vance argues that the legal drinking age in the United States should not differ from the age of majority and, ideally, should not be regulated by the federal government. Vance notes that the drinking age was raised from eighteen to twenty-one by the National Minimum Drinking Age Act of 1984, legislation that he argues contains numerous flaws. Vance is a columnist and policy adviser for the Future of Freedom Foundation, an associated scholar of the Ludwig von Mises Institute, and author of The War on Drugs Is a War on Freedom.

Last month [May 2013], the parliament in Turkey passed legislation ostensibly designed to curb alcohol consumption among Turkish youth.

Restrictive Laws Regarding Alcohol

Retailers may not sell alcohol between 10 P.M. and 6 A.M. No alcohol may be sold within 100 meters of educational or religious centers. Educational and health institutions, sports clubs, and gas stations will be banned from selling alcohol. Although the advertising of alcohol is already illegal, the new law forces TV stations to blur images of alcoholic beverages shown on the screen. All liquor bottles must display warning signs about the dangers of consuming alcohol. There will also be stricter penalties for drunken driving.

"We don't want a generation walking around drunk night and day. We want a youth that is sharp and shrewd and full of knowledge," said Turkey's prime minister, Recep Tayyip Erdogan, in defense of the legislation. The Turkish president signed the legislation into law on June 10.

Yet even with those restrictions on alcohol sales, residents of Bridgewater, Connecticut, who want to purchase alcohol would

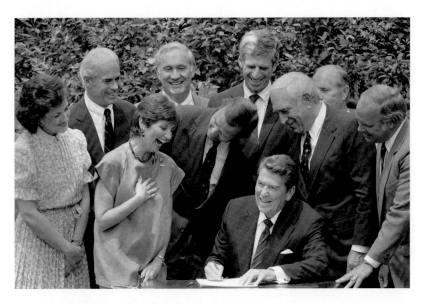

President Ronald Reagan signs legislation raising the national drinking age to twenty-one in 1984. The United States is one of only three developed countries in the world with a drinking age over eighteen. © AP Photo.

have an easier time in Turkey than in their own town—the last remaining "dry" town in Connecticut. But Connecticut is not alone; thirty-two other states have laws that allow counties and local jurisdictions to prohibit the sale of alcohol. Three of those states—Kansas, Mississippi, and Tennessee—are "dry" by default; individual counties must vote to become "wet." More than half of the 75 counties in Arkansas are "dry." There are 35 municipalities in New Jersey that prohibit the retail sale of alcohol. The county in Tennessee where the Jack Daniel's distillery is located is a "dry" county!

Although every state in the Union has its own peculiar laws regarding the sale, possession, manufacturing, and consumption of alcohol, there is one thing that is uniform throughout the country—the drinking age of 21.

Why is the drinking age 21?

The Drinking Age in the United States

The United States is one of only three developed countries in the world with a nationwide drinking age over 18. The other two countries are Iceland and Japan, which both have a drinking age of 20.

The main problem with the United States's having a drinking age of 21 is that the age of majority is 18 (19 in Alabama and Nebraska), as it is throughout most of the world. That is the age when a person assumes the legal rights and responsibilities of an adult. Thus, anyone in the United States who has reached the age of 18 is legally eligible to vote, run for office, enter legally binding contracts, marry, engage in consensual sex with other adults, adopt children, join the military, be subject to the draft (when the draft is in force), purchase tobacco (except in Alabama, Alaska, New Jersey and Utah, where one must be 19), and purchase pornography; that is, everything under the sun except buy a beer.

Whether the age of majority should be higher, lower, or kept at age 18 is irrelevant. Whatever the age of majority, it makes absolutely no sense for it to be lower than the drinking age. In most countries, the age of majority coincides with the drinking age.

So why is the drinking age 21 in the United States?

Before Prohibition (1919), which prohibited only the manufacture, sale, and transportation of alcohol, not the drinking of it, only a handful of states even had a legal drinking age. After the repeal of Prohibition (1933), all of the states gradually established a minimum age to purchase alcohol. The most common age was 21. After the Twenty-Sixth Amendment to the Constitution was adopted in 1971, which prohibited the states from setting their voting age above 18, most states lowered their drinking ages, usually down to 18. From the late 1970s to the early 1980s, some states raised their drinking ages to 19, 20, or even 21. But by mid-1988, every state in the Union had raised its drinking age to 21.

Why is that? Why is the drinking age 21?

The Problem of Drunk Driving

The answer is the National Minimum Drinking Age Act of 1984, which mandated that the states raise their drinking ages to 21 or their federal highway funding would be cut by 10 percent beginning in fiscal year 1988.

On April 14, 1982, Ronald Reagan issued Executive Order 12358 establishing the Presidential Commission on Drunk Driving. The commission was composed of twenty-six members appointed by the president plus two members of Congress from each House. The functions of the commission were to:

a. heighten public awareness of the seriousness of the drunk driving problem;

b. persuade States and communities to attack the drunk driving problem in a more organized and systematic manner, including plans to eliminate bottlenecks in the arrest, trial and sentencing process that impair the effectiveness of many drunk driving laws;

Drunk Driving Around the World

In terms of alcohol-impaired driving and related fatalities, a recent NHTSA [National Highway Traffic Safety Administration] study that compared DUI [driving under the influence] laws in the United States to those in comparable nations, such as the European Union States, Canada, Australia, New Zealand, Japan, and Brazil, found that the United States had the highest proportion of traffic fatalities that were alcohol-related among the 12 countries reporting data. The same study found that the United States has the highest legal BAC [blood alcohol content] limit for impaired driving—.10 at the time of publication (2000)—and relatively lax enforcement as compared to nations like Australia, New Zealand, Sweden, and Spain where mandatory random breath testing and sobriety checkpoints were reported to be frequent and prevalent. The legal drinking age of all countries in the report was 18, with Japan and Canada being the only exceptions. Japan sets 20 as its legal limit, while the legal drinking age in Canada is 19 in all provinces except for Alberta, Quebec, and Manitoba, where people can drink legally at age 18.

Choose Responsibility, "Frequently Asked Questions." www.chooseresponsibility.org.

c. encourage State and local officials and organizations to accept and use the latest techniques and methods to solve the problem; and

d. generate public support for increased enforcement of State and local drunk driving laws.

Although the commission was supposed to exist for one year, Reagan signed another executive order extending the term of the commission to December 31, 1983.

On December 13, 1982, "An Interim Report to the Nation from the President's Commission on Drunk Driving" was released. It recommended that "States should immediately adopt 21 years of age as the minimum legal drinking age for all alcoholic beverages." In a statement issued on April 5, 1983, Reagan noted this recommendation and informed the public that three states had already raised their legal drinking age. The commission's final report was issued in November of 1983 prefaced by a letter from Reagan stating that drunk driving was "a national menace, a national tragedy, and a national disgrace." The commission's eighth recommendation (out of 39), "Minimum Legal Purchasing Age," was not only that the states should raise their drinking age, but that:

> Legislation at the Federal level should be enacted providing that each State enact and/or maintain a law requiring 21 years as the minimum legal age for purchasing and possessing all alcoholic beverages. Such legislation should provide that the Secretary of the United States Department of Transportation disapprove any project under Section 106 of the Federal Aid Highway Act (Title 23, United States Code) for any State not having and enforcing such a law.

The National Minimum Drinking Age Act

Reagan signed into law the National Minimum Drinking Age Act on July 17, 1984. It had been passed in the House by voice vote, passed in the Senate with an amendment by voice vote, and then agreed to in the House by unanimous consent; that is, it had no measurable opposition in either House of Congress. In an official statement, the president said he was convinced that the bill would "help persuade State legislators to act in the national interest to save our children's lives, by raising the drinking age to 21 across the country."

There have been some major criticisms leveled at this legislation:

1. That the exclusive interest in raising the drinking age marginalized the 38 other recommendations in the commission's final report.

2. That the majority of 18–20-year-olds choose to ignore the law and drink anyway, which meant that in many cases they drank unsafely and irresponsibly in clandestine locations to avoid prosecution.

3. That alcohol-related automobile accidents were already in decline before the adoption of the legislation.

4. That for alcohol-related fatalities not associated with automobiles, raising the drinking age to 21 has had no discernible effect on fatalities associated with alcohol.

5. That safer cars, higher awareness by drivers of all ages, greater utilization of a "designated driver," and more vigorous law enforcement are what had led to the decline of driving fatalities associated with alcohol.

The Role of Government

There is another criticism of the National Minimum Drinking Age Act that has rarely been vocalized: it is incompatible with individual liberty and limited government—the things that Republicans in the Congress and the presidency at the time professed to believe.

First, it is not the federal government's business to prevent any legal adult of any age from purchasing alcohol. If a drinking age of 21 prevents highway deaths of those who are 18–20, then the same argument could be made that a drinking age of 25 would prevent highway deaths of those who are 18–24. But why stop there? If reducing highway deaths is the priority, and if merely raising the drinking age reduces highway deaths, then it follows that the government should just ban alcohol altogether—something that few Americans would be willing to accept no matter how many highway deaths it would be claimed to prevent. And second, it is not the federal government's business to dictate to the states. Under our constitutional system of federalism, it is actually the other way around.

Libertarians would go even further.

- It is not the proper role of the federal government to seek ways to reduce highway alcohol-related fatalities.
- It is not the proper role of the federal government to discourage anyone from drinking alcohol.
- It is not the proper role of the federal government to set a minimum age to purchase, possess, or drink alcohol.
- It is not the proper role of the federal government to license businesses to sell alcohol.
- It is not the proper role of the federal government to have a Bureau of Alcohol, Tobacco, Firearms and Explosives.
- It is not the proper role of the federal government to give states highway funds.
- It is not the proper role of the federal government to have a Department of Transportation.

In a free society, it is the role of businesses, parents, friends, family, religious organizations, temperance unions, social-welfare groups, medical professionals, and others to instruct the young on the potential dangers and safe use of alcohol; that is, anyone but the government.

| *"The evidence strongly suggests that setting the minimum legal drinking age at 21 is better from a cost and benefit perspective than setting it at 18."*

There Is Good Reason for Allowing Emancipation Prior to Legal Drinking

Christopher Carpenter and Carlos Dobkin

In the following viewpoint, Christopher Carpenter and Carlos Dobkin consider the evidence in favor of various legislative proposals to lower the drinking age. They argue that the evidence suggests that lowering the drinking age from twenty-one years of age to eighteen would result in an increase in harms, where the economic value of such harms is larger than the value assigned additional drinking. Carpenter is associate professor of economics and public policy at The Paul Merage School of Business at the University of California, Irvine, and Dobkin is an associate professor of economics at the University of California, Santa Cruz.

In summer 2008, more than 100 college presidents and other higher education officials signed the Amethyst Initiative, which calls for a reexamination of the minimum legal drinking age in the United States. The current age-21 limit in the United States is higher than in Canada (18 or 19, depending on the province), Mexico (18), and most western European countries (typically 16 or 18). A central argument of the Amethyst Initiative is that the U.S. minimum legal drinking age policy results in more dangerous drinking than would occur if the legal drinking age were lower. A companion organization called Choose Responsibility—led in part by Amethyst Initiative founder John McCardell, former Middlebury College president—explicitly proposes "a series of changes that will allow 18–20 year-olds to purchase, possess and consume alcoholic beverages."

Balancing Harms and Benefits of Lowering the Drinking Age

Fueled in part by the high-profile national media attention garnered by the Amethyst Initiative and Choose Responsibility, activists and policymakers in several states, including Kentucky, Wisconsin, South Carolina, Missouri, South Dakota, Minnesota, and Vermont, have put forth various legislative proposals to lower their state's drinking age from 21 to 18, though no state has adopted a lower minimum legal drinking age yet.

Does the age-21 drinking limit in the United States reduce alcohol consumption by young adults and its harms, or as the signatories of the Amethyst Initiative contend, is it "not working"? Alcohol consumption and its harms are extremely common among young adults. According to results from the 2006–2007 National Health Interview Survey, adults age 18–25 report that on average they drank on 36 days in the previous year and typically consumed 5.1 drinks on the days they drank. If consumed at a single sitting, five drinks meets the clinical definition of "binge" or "heavy episodic" drinking. This consumption contributes to a substantial public health problem: five drinks for a 160-pound man with a limited time between drinks leads to a blood alcohol concentration of about 0.12 percent and results in moderate to severe impairments in coordination, concentration, reflexes, reaction time, depth perception, and peripheral vision. For comparison, the legal limit for driving in the United States is generally 0.08 percent blood alcohol content. Not surprisingly, motor vehicle accidents (the leading cause of death and injury in this age group), homicides, suicides, falls, and other accidents are all strongly associated with alcohol consumption. Because around 80 percent of deaths among young adults are due to these "external" causes (as opposed to cancer, infectious disease, or other "internal" causes), policies that change the ways in and extent to which young people consume alcohol have the potential to affect the mortality rate of this population substantially.

In this paper, we summarize a large and compelling body of empirical evidence which shows that one of the central claims of the signatories of the Amethyst Initiative is incorrect: setting the minimum legal drinking age at 21 clearly reduces alcohol consumption and its major harms. However, this finding alone is not a sufficient justification for the current minimum legal drinking age, in part because it does not take into account the benefits of alcohol consumption. To put it another way, it is likely that restricting the alcohol consumption of people in their late 20s (or even older) would also reduce alcohol-related harms at least modestly. However, given the much lower rate at which adults in this age group experience alcohol-related harms, their utility from drinking likely outweighs the associated costs. Thus, when considering at what age to set the minimum legal drinking age, we need to determine if the reduction in alcohol-related harms justifies the reduction in consumer surplus that results from preventing people from consuming alcohol. . . .

Determining an Optimal Drinking Age Is Difficult

Alcohol consumption by young adults results in numerous harms including deaths, injuries, commission of crime, criminal victimization, risky sexual behavior, and reduced workforce

John McCardell, right, watches as David Jernigan testifies before the legislature in Montpelier, Vermont, in 2010. McCardell is head of Choose Responsibility, an organization that argues states should be able to lower the drinking age. © AP Photo/Toby Talbot.

productivity. A substantial portion of these harms are either directly imposed on other individuals (as is the case with crime) or largely transferred to society as a whole through insurance markets as is the case with injuries. In addition, there is the theoretical possibility (supported by laboratory evidence) that youths may discount future utility too heavily, underestimate the future harm of their current behavior, and/or mispredict how they will feel about their choices in the future. If this is the case, even risks that are borne directly by the drinker are not being fully taken into account when an individual is deciding how much alcohol to consume. Given that young adults are imposing costs on others and probably not fully taking into account their own cost of alcohol consumption, there is a case for government intervention targeting their alcohol consumption. The minimum legal drinking age represents one approach to reducing drinking by young adults.

Determining the optimal age at which to set the minimum legal drinking age requires estimates of the loss in consumer surplus that results from reducing peoples' alcohol consumption. It also requires estimating the benefits to the drinker and to others from reducing alcohol-related harms. Unfortunately, it is not possible to obtain credible estimates of these key parameters at every point in the age distribution. First, there are no credible estimates of the effects of drinking ages lower than 18 or higher than 21 because the minimum legal drinking age has not been set outside this range in a significant portion of the United States since the 1930s, and the countries with current drinking ages outside this range look very different from the United States. In fact . . . even estimating the effects on adverse outcomes of a drinking age in the 18 to 21 range is challenging. Second, we lack good ways to estimate the consumer surplus loss that results from restricting drinking, a problem that has characterized the entire literature on optimal alcohol control and taxation. . . .

Estimating the Effects of a Drinking Age of Eighteen

Thus, rather than try to estimate the optimal age at which to set the minimum legal drinking age, we focus on an analysis that is more feasible and useful from a policy perspective. The drinking age in the United States is currently 21, and there is no push to raise it. If it is lowered, there are many reasons to believe it will most likely be lowered to 18. First, the primary effort by activists for a lower drinking age is to lower the age to 18, either on its own or in conjunction with other alcohol-control initiatives such as education programs. In fact, 18 was the most commonly chosen age among the states that adopted lower minimum legal drinking ages in the 1970s. Second, 18 is the age of majority for other important activities such as voting, military service, and serving on juries, thus making it a natural focal point (though notably many states set different minimum ages for a variety of other activities such as driving, consenting to sexual activity, gambling, and purchasing handguns). Finally, many other countries have set their minimum legal drinking age at 18.

Because a change in the drinking age is likely to involve lowering it from 21 to 18, we focus on estimating the effect of lowering the drinking age by this amount on alcohol consumption, costs borne by the drinker, and costs borne by other people. Alcohol consumption can result in harms through many different channels. The effects of age-based drinking restrictions on long-term harms are very hard to estimate so we focus on the major acute harms that result from alcohol consumption including: deaths, nonfatal injuries, and crime. We pay particular attention to the effect of the drinking age on mortality because mortality is well-measured, has been the outcome focused on by much of the previous research on this topic, and is arguably the most costly of alcohol-related harms. To avoid the difficulty of trying to estimate the increase in consumer surplus that results from allowing people to drink, we estimate how much drinking is likely to increase if the drinking age is lowered from 21 to 18 and compare this to the likely increase in harms to the drinker and to other people. This allows us to characterize the harms in terms of dollars per drink. Since we are missing some of the acute harms and all of the long-term harms of alcohol consumption, the estimates we present in this paper are lower bounds of the costs associated with each drink.

Adding how much the drinker paid for the drink to the cost per drink borne by the drinker yields a lower bound on how much a person would have to value the drink for its consumption to be the result of a fully informed and rational choice. The per-drink cost borne by people other than the drinker provides a lower bound on the externality cost. If the externality cost is large or if the total cost of a drink (costs imposed on others plus costs the drinker bears privately plus the price of the drink itself) is larger than what we believe the value of the drink is to the person consuming it, then this would suggest that the higher drinking age is justified. . . .

Increased Risk of Death for the Drinker

When considering whether it makes sense to lower the drinking age from 21 to 18 the critical issue is determining whether the increase in consumer surplus that results from allowing 18–20 year-olds to drink is large enough to justify the increase in alcohol-related harms. The most direct way to make this comparison is to estimate the change in consumer surplus and compare it to the increase in harms as measured in dollars. However, it is very challenging to credibly estimate the consumer surplus associated with the additional drinks that 18–20 year-olds would consume if the drinking age were lowered to 18. For this reason we implement an alternative approach of estimating the harm per drink to the person consuming the drink and the harm per drink imposed on other people.

The greatest immediate cost to the individual of an additional drink is that it increases their risk of dying. The estimates . . . suggest that if the drinking age were lowered to 18, there would be an additional 8 deaths per 100,000 person-years for the 18–20 age group. A common estimate of the value of a statistical life is $8.72 million (converted to 2009 U.S. dollars). This suggests that for every 100,000 young adults allowed to drink legally for a year, the cost in terms of increased mortality is about $70 million (8 × $8.72 million). Given that we estimate an increase of 4.56 million drinks for every 100,000 person-years, this suggests that the hidden cost of each drink due to the increased mortality risk is over $15 (70/4.56). Given that each drink potentially has other adverse impacts on the individual, such as injuries, reduced productivity, and reduced health, this estimate is a lower bound.

INCREASES IN MORTALITY RATES BY CAUSE AT AGE TWENTY-ONE

Deaths per 100,000

Cause		Increase at Age 21	Standard Error	Mortality Rate
All Causes		8.06	[2.17]	93.07
Internal Causes		0.66	[1.01]	20.07
External Causes	Suicide	2.37	[0.76]	11.70
	Motor Vehicle Accident	3.65	[1.25]	29.81
	Homicide	−0.10	[0.58]	17.60
	Alcohol	0.41	[0.21]	0.99
	Other External	1.37	[0.77]	13.40

Taken from: Christopher Carpenter and Carlos Dobkin, "The Minimum Legal Drinking Age and Public Health," *Journal of Economic Perspectives*, vol. 25, no. 2, Spring 2011.

Increased Risks to Others

The costs of the reduction in the minimum legal drinking age borne by people other than those consuming the drink come from many sources: we focus on three of the major ones. The first external cost includes the risk that an individual will be killed by a drinker in a motor vehicle accident. Our best estimate is that the typical young adult killed while driving drunk kills another person 21 percent of the time. This suggests that lowering the drinking age will kill at least an additional 0.77 people (3.65 drivers killed in motor vehicle accidents . . . . $\times$ 0.21) annually for every 100,000 18–20 year-olds allowed to drink. Using the value of a statistical life from above, this is a cost of $6.7 million (8.72 $\times$ 0.77 = 6.7) for every 100,000 people allowed to drink after the drinking age is lowered. This estimate is a lower bound, because it does not include the people killed where the drunk driver survives. The second external cost is due to the increased risk that a drinker will commit robbery or assault. The best available estimate suggests that lowering the drinking age will result in 63 additional arrests for assault and 8 additional arrests for robbery annually for every 100,000 newly legal drinkers. Given that not every crime results in an arrest, these two estimates need to be rescaled by the proportion of reported assaults and robberies that are cleared by an arrest, which are 54 and 25 percent, respectively. At an estimated cost of $20,500 per assault and $17,800 per robbery (converted to 2009 U.S. dollars), the crime cost imposed on others is $2,400,000 ($20,500 $\times$ 63/0.54 $\approx$ $2,400,000) for assaults and $656,000 ($17,800 $\times$ 8/0.25 $\approx$ $570,000) for robberies. A third external cost is that the drinker will injure themselves and require medical treatment. If the medical care is covered by insurance or if the costs are absorbed by the hospital, these costs are effectively borne by people other than the drinker. The 408 additional emergency department visits and 77 additional hospital stays per 100,000 person-years that would likely occur if the drinking age were lowered impose a substantial cost: the average cost of an alcohol-related emergency department visit is $3,387, and the average cost of an alcohol-related inpatient hospital stay is $12,562 for a total cost per 100,000 person-years of $2.35 million [(3,387 × 408) + (12,562 × 77)]. Summing these externality costs gives a total cost of about $12.02 million per 100,000 person-years (that is, $6.7 million + $2.4 million + $0.57 million + $2.35 million = $12.02 million). Dividing this estimate by the change in the number of drinks yields an externality cost of $2.63 ($12.02/4.56) per drink. Given that there are numerous alcohol-related harms not included in this calculation, this is a downward-biased estimate of the cost that the drinker imposes on others.

Not Worth the Cost

The estimates above suggest that the total cost of a drink to the person drinking it is at least $15 plus what the person paid for the drink. It is unlikely that the average drinker values a drink this highly. This finding suggests that the drinker is not fully aware of the personal costs of their behavior and there is a role for government intervention. Moreover, with each drink there are costs imposed on others of at least $2.63, which again suggests a role for government intervention to deal with this externality. These estimates clearly suggest that lowering the drinking age will lead to an increase in harms that is very likely larger than the value that people put on the additional drinking.

Our focus here has been on predicting the effects of lowering the minimum drinking age, but of course, a lower drinking age might be combined with other policies like mandatory alcohol licensing (similar to driver licensing) and relevant, reality-based alcohol education, both of which are advocated by the Choose Responsibility group. Although the research summarized here convinces us that an earlier drinking age alone would increase alcohol-related harms, we do not think there is enough evidence to evaluate the effectiveness of alcohol education and alcohol licensing, either in isolation or in combination with a lower minimum drinking age. While we are certainly not opposed to experimentation with alternative policies for encouraging responsible alcohol consumption, the evidence strongly suggests that setting the minimum legal drinking age at 21 is better from a cost and benefit perspective than setting it at 18 and that any proposal to reduce the drinking age should face a very high burden of proof.

| *"The age of majority and the age of competence are coming apart."*

The Mind-Booty Problem: Rethinking the Age of Sexual Consent

William Saletan

In the following viewpoint, William Saletan argues that the age of legal consent for sex should be lowered. Saletan contends that the current age of consent in many localities in the United States results in the same treatment in the criminal justice system for people who engage in consensual sex with minors and for pedophiles. Saletan argues that a logical scheme for regulating teen sex would take into account participants' cognitive and emotional competence to consent and that penalties for sexual activity should be developmentally appropriate as well. Saletan writes about politics, science, technology, and other topics for Slate.

In Georgia, 21-year-old Genarlow Wilson is serving a mandatory 10-year jail sentence for aggravated child molestation. His crime: When he was 17, he had oral sex with a 15-year-old girl. In Utah, polygamist leader Warren Jeffs has been convicted as an accomplice to rape for orchestrating a sexually coercive marriage between a 14-year-old girl and her 19-year-old cousin. In Michigan, a 53-year-old prosecutor is in custody on charges of entering the state to have sex with a 5-year-old girl.

Earlier Puberty Is Leading to Earlier Sex

This is the reality of sex with minors: The ages of the parties vary widely from case to case. For more than a century, states and countries have been raising and standardizing the legal age of consent. Horny teenagers are being thrown in with pedophiles. The point of this crackdown was to lock up perverts and protect incompetent minors. But the rationales and the numbers don't match up. The age of majority and the age of competence are coming apart. The age of competence is fracturing, and the age of female puberty is declining. It's time to abandon the myth of the "age of consent" and lower the threshold for legal sex.

The original age of consent, codified in English common law and later adopted by the American colonies, ranged from 10 to 12. In 1885, Britain and the states began raising the age to 16, ostensibly to protect girls' natural innocence. This moral idea was later bolstered by scientific reference to the onset of puberty.

But the age of puberty has been going the other way. Over the past 150 years in the United States and Europe, the average age of menarche—a girl's first period—has fallen two to four months per decade, depending on the country. In 1840, the age was 15.3 years. By the early 1980s, it was 12.8. At first, the trend was driven by nutrition, sanitation, and disease control. Recently, some analysts thought it had stopped. But dietary changes and obesity may be pushing it forward again. Two years ago, researchers reported that the average age of menarche among American girls, which had declined from 12 years and 9 months in the 1960s to 12 years and 6 months in the 1990s, was down to 12 years and 4 months by the

---

beginning of this decade. Among black girls, average menarche was occurring about three weeks after their 12th birthday.

Getting your period doesn't mean having sex right away. But earlier puberty does, on average, mean earlier sex. According to the most recent data from the U.S. government's Youth Risk Behavior Survey, one of every three American ninth graders has had intercourse. And that's not counting the millions of teens who have had oral sex instead.

Cognitive and Emotional Competence to Consent

Having sex at 12 is a bad idea. But if you're pubescent, it might be, in part, *your* bad idea. Conversely, having sex with a 12-year-old, when you're 20, is scummy. But it doesn't necessarily make you the kind of predator who has to be locked up. A guy who goes after 5-year-old girls is deeply pathological. A guy who goes after a womanly body that happens to be 13 years old is failing to regulate a natural attraction. That doesn't excuse him. But it does justify treating him differently.

I'm not saying 12 should be the official age of "consent." Consent implies competence, and 12-year-olds don't really have that. In a forthcoming review of studies, Laurence Steinberg of Temple University observes that at ages 12 to 13, only 11 percent of kids score at an average (50th percentile) adult level on tests of intellectual ability. By ages 14 to 15, the percentage has doubled to 21. By ages 16 to 17, it has doubled again to 42. After that, it levels off.

By that standard, the age of consent should be 16. But competence isn't just cognitive. It's emotional, too. Steinberg reports that on tests of psychosocial maturity, kids are much slower to develop. From ages 10 to 21, only one of every four young people scores at an average adult level. By ages 22 to 25, one in three reaches that level. By ages 26 to 30, it's up to two in three.

Steinberg concludes that "risk-taking increases between childhood and adolescence as a result of changes around the

© Alfredo Martirena/Cartoonstock.com

time of puberty in the brain's socio-emotional system." In tests, these tendencies peak from ages 13 to 16. Subsequently, "[r]isk-taking declines between adolescence and adulthood because of changes in the brain's cognitive control system—changes which improve individuals' capacity for self-regulation." The latter kind of competence doesn't reach adult levels until the mid-20s.

A Logical Scheme to Regulate Teen Sex

Lay out these numbers on a timeline, and you have the beginnings of a logical scheme for regulating teen sex. First comes the age at which your brain wants sex and your body signals to others that you're ready for it. Then comes the age of cognitive competence. Then comes the age of emotional competence. Each of these thresholds should affect our expectations, and the expectations should apply to the older party in a relationship as well as to the younger one. The older you get, the higher the standard to which you should be held responsible.

The lowest standard is whether the partner you're targeting is sexually developed as an object. If her body is childlike, you're seriously twisted. But if it's womanly, and you're too young to think straight, maybe we'll cut you some slack.

Genarlow Wilson displays the Supreme Court of Georgia's decision that released him from prison in 2007. He was given a ten year sentence for oral sex with a fifteen year old when he was seventeen. © AP Photo/Gregory Smith.

The next standard is whether your target is intellectually developed as a subject. We're not talking about her body anymore; we're talking about her mind. When you were younger, we cut you slack for thinking only about boobs. But now we expect you to think about whether she's old enough to judge the physical and emotional risks of messing around. The same standards apply, in reverse, if you're a woman.

It's possible that you'll think about these things but fail to restrain yourself. If you're emotionally immature, we'll take that into consideration. But once you cross the third line, the age of self-regulatory competence, we'll throw the book at you.

What do "cutting slack" and "throwing the book" mean? If you're young, we could let your parents handle it. We could assign a social service agency to check up on you. We could require you to get counseling. We could issue a restraining order. We could put you on probation. We could put you in a juvenile facility, a mental institution, or jail. In the worst case, we could subject you to a mandatory minimum sentence.

Whatever the particulars, the measures taken should be developmentally appropriate. "Age-span" provisions, which currently allow for sex with somebody near your own age, are a good start, but they're not objectively grounded. That's why they differ wildly from state to state. I'd draw the object line at 12, the cognitive line at 16, and the self-regulatory line at 25. I'd lock up anyone who went after a 5-year-old. I'd come down hard on a 38-year-old who married a 15-year-old. And if I ran a college, I'd discipline professors for sleeping with freshmen. When you're 35, "she's legal" isn't good enough.

What I wouldn't do is slap a mandatory sentence on a 17-year-old, even if his nominal girlfriend were 12. I know the idea of sex at that age is hard to stomach. I wish our sexual, cognitive, and emotional maturation converged in a magic moment we could call the age of consent. But they don't.

15

"Even as students arrive to campus as adults in the technical sense, colleges and universities are pressured to assume greater responsibility for them."

For Many College Students, Home Means Both the Place They Live and the Place They Left

Timothy L. Hulsey

In the following viewpoint, Timothy L. Hulsey argues that although college students have normally reached the age of majority—thus technically emancipated from their parents and officially adults—they are increasingly overprotected by both their parents and their schools. Hulsey contends that this change has been brought about by a change in parents, who now expect colleges to look after their children and be responsive to parental requests. Hulsey is the associate provost of the Chancellor's Honors and Haslam Scholars programs at the University of Tennessee, Knoxville.

Most students reach the age of majority as they begin higher education, but being legally accountable for their actions has not led to increased freedoms for them. Rather, recent years have seen the surprising return of an old notion: *in loco parentis,* Latin for "instead of or in place of a parent." Even as students arrive to campus as adults in a technical sense, colleges and universities are pressured to assume greater responsibility for them. The transition, then, from family home to undergraduate living can be difficult for all parties: students, parents, and schools.

Dennis Black, head of university life and services at State University of New York in Buffalo, saw these developments coming. He observed in 2000:

> Although students arrive for higher education today as adults, student affairs professionals are being asked to prepare them to deal quickly with adult responsibilities. The campus is quite different than it was when baby boomer parents of today's traditional students were in college. In decades gone by, campus life was highly regulated and regimented by the college or university. The campus exercised control over student life and experiences. Today, students have much more legal and social responsibility for themselves, their education, and their lives. In the past, the college was the adult influence in student college lives. Today, students themselves are the adults, with rights and responsibilities derived both from campus and community codes. In these times, colleges and universities are being asked to assume greater responsibility for students and their behavior at a time when it would seem higher education should be exercising less concern and control.

Many students expect oversight from their parents and school. As Bradley University's Alan Galsky and Joyce Shotick note recently in *The Chronicle of Higher Education,* millennial parents are "very active in calling or e-mailing their children's professors, as well as college administrators and staff, with their concerns. While such calls have always taken place to a limited extent, they now occur on a daily basis—with the knowledge and approval of the student." For example, a parent demanded that a

The Danger of Over-Controlling Parents

Blame it on technology or anxiety or habit—some parents remain so involved that they are leaving their college-age kids anxious, depressed, and ill-equipped to deal with matters both small and large, according to experts.

One study, published online in February [2013] in the *Journal of Child and Family Studies*, found that over-controlling parents undermine the competence and confidence of college students and can negatively affect the parent-student relationship.

> Bella English, "'Snowplow Parents' Overly
> Involved in College Students' Lives,"
> Boston Globe, *November 9, 2013.*
> *www.bostonglobe.com.*

university "provide technical computer support 24 hours a day because her daughter had electronically 'lost' a term paper at 3 A.M. that was due later that morning."

"Velcro parents," those unwilling or unable to let go of their children, facilitate this ongoing dependence. "Some undergraduate officials see in parents' separation anxieties evidence of the excesses of modern child-rearing," writes Trip Gabriel for *The New York Times*. "A good deal of it has to do with the evolution of overinvolvement in our students' lives," explains W. Houston Dougharty, steward of student affairs at Grinnell College. "These are the baby-on-board parents," Dougharty elaborates to Gabriel, "highly invested in their students' success." The result is a generational sea change, declares Sue Wasiolek, dean of students at Duke University. "It's ironic that the students who wanted to eliminate any kind of parental role that the university played—making them sign in and out of dorms, for example—have be-

Carly Turro moves into her dorm room at Colgate University with the help of her parents Fiona, left, and Joe. Some believe that overprotective parents and schools may leave students unprepared for adult life. © AP Photo/Kevin Rivoli.

come parents who demand to be involved in their children's lives," she comments in "Helicopter Parents," Bridget Booher's article for *Duke Magazine* a few years ago.

These same parents "now insist that colleges take responsibility for the actions of their millennial children due to the 'special relationship' that they believe forms upon enrollment," echoes Joseph Storch, a specialist in student affairs for State University of New York's counsel office. Parents, often paying significant tuition bills, "want to be their children's advocates to ensure that the college meets what they believe to be its obligations. They want access to administrators, and more often than in the past they want to hold the colleges accountable if their children are harmed or do not succeed," points out Wendy S. White, Penn's general counsel, in a December 2005 piece in *The Chronicle of Higher Education.*

Having grown up with parents involved in their every decision, students come to college assuming their parents and the schools will look out for them. The danger, of course, is that the students may leave campus unprepared for independent adult life.

Of equal concern is that overprotected students won't develop minds of their own. As the author of a September 1993 opinion piece in Duke University's student-run newspaper, *The Chronicle*, presaged:

> College students are not children. They are adults, here for an education. Some may be immature, or overly affected by peer pressure, social groups or advertising. A few might benefit from working a month on an assembly line. But they are not children; in general, they are open to new ideas, capable of responsibility and do not require constant supervision. . . . I still may be young enough and naïve enough myself to believe in the power of individuals to make their own decisions. Frankly, I see no real alternative—unless you're willing to accept unquestioning conformity as a way of life.

Organizations to Contact

The editors have compiled the following list of organizations concerned with the issues debated in this book. The descriptions are derived from materials provided by the organizations. All have publications or information available for interested readers. The list was compiled on the date of publication of the present volume; the information provided here may change. Be aware that many organizations take several weeks or longer to respond to inquiries, so allow as much time as possible.

Advocates for Youth

2000 M Street, NW, Suite 750
Washington, DC 20036
(202) 419-3420 • fax: (202) 419-1448
website: www.advocatesforyouth.org

Advocates for Youth is an organization that works both in the United States and in developing countries to inform young people aged 14–25 about reproductive and sexual health and encourage them to make responsible decisions. The group believes that youth deserve accurate, confidential information about sex and reproduction. Advocates for Youth publishes numerous informational essays available at its website, including "Meeting the Needs of Every Student."

American Center for Law and Justice (ACLJ)

P.O. Box 90555
Washington, DC 20090-0555
(800) 296-4529
website: www.aclj.org

The American Center for Law and Justice (ACLJ) is dedicated to protecting religious freedom, which it views as a God-given right, in the United States and worldwide. It litigates, advocates, provides free legal services, and offers advice to individuals and governments concerning many issues. The group has represented clients before the US Supreme Court and in other federal courts. ACLJ has numerous memos, position papers, and radio recordings available at its website, including "Birth Control and Minors."

American Civil Liberties Union (ACLU)
125 Broad Street, 18th Floor
New York, NY 10004
(212) 549-2500
website: www.aclu.com

The American Civil Liberties Union (ACLU) is a national organization whose mission is to defend Americans' civil rights as guaranteed in the US Constitution and laws. The ACLU works in courts, legislatures, and communities to guarantee First Amendment rights, the right to equal protection, the right to due process, and the right to privacy. The ACLU publishes the semi-annual newsletter *Civil Liberties Alert* as well as briefing papers supporting abortion rights and access to birth control, among other reproductive health issues. The ACLU publishes and distributes numerous policy statements and reports, including the fact sheet "Overview of Lesbian and Gay Parenting, Adoption, and Foster Care."

Cato Institute
1000 Massachusetts Ave., NW
Washington, DC 20001-5403
(202) 842-0200 • fax: (202) 842-3490
website: www.cato.org

The Cato Institute is a public policy research foundation dedicated to limiting the role of government, protecting individual liberties, and promoting free markets. The institute commissions a variety of publications, including books, monographs, briefing papers and other studies. Among its publications are the quarterly magazine *Regulation*, the bimonthly *Cato Policy Report*, and articles such as "Schools Shouldn't Play Doctor."

Center for Reproductive Rights
120 Wall Street
New York, NY 10005
(917) 637-3600 • fax: (917) 637-3666
e-mail: info@reprorights.org
website: www.reproductiverights.org

The Center for Reproductive Rights is a global legal advocacy organization dedicated to reproductive freedom, which it views as a basic human right that governments worldwide must protect and advance. The group litigates inside and outside the US, engages policymakers regarding reproductive rights, and trains lawyers worldwide. The Center for Reproductive Rights publishes articles, reports, and briefing papers, among which is the article "Parental Involvement Laws."

Concerned Women for America (CWA)
1015 Fifteenth Street, NW, Suite 1100
Washington, D.C. 20005
(202) 488-7000 • fax: (202) 488-0806
website: www.cwfa.org

Concerned Women for America (CWA) is a public policy women's organization focused on promoting Biblical values and combating secularism among citizens and in the public sphere through prayer, education, and action. The group's core issues include sanctity of life, defense of family, education, religious liberty, national sovereignty, sexual exploitation, and support for Israel. Among the organization's brochures, fact sheets, and articles available on its website is "Protecting Parental Rights from Activist Judges."

Focus on the Family
8605 Explorer Drive
Colorado Springs, CO 80920-1051
(719) 531-5181
website: www.focusonthefamily.com

Focus on the Family is a Christian organization that works to nurture and defend what it views as the God-ordained institution of the family. The organization works to promote the permanence of marriage, the sanctity of human life, and the value of male and female sexuality. Among the many publications the organization produces is the article "Adoption from Foster Care."

Guttmacher Institute
125 Maiden Lane, 7th Floor
New York, NY 10038
(212) 248-1111 • fax: (212) 248-1951
website: www.guttmacher.org

The Guttmacher Institute conducts social science research, educates the public, and performs policy analysis with the goal of protecting and ensuring sexual and reproductive health and rights around the world. It researches sexual activity, contraception, abortion, and childbearing, publishes three journals, and offers extensive information on its website. The Institute's monthly publications *State Policies in Brief* provide information on legislative and judicial actions affecting reproductive health, such as the recent brief "An Overview of Minors' Consent Law."

National Center for Youth Law (NCYL)
405 Fourteenth Street, 15th Floor
Oakland, CA 94612
(510) 835-8098 fax: (510) 835-8099
e-mail: info@youthlaw.org

The National Center for Youth Law (NCYL) legislates on behalf of low-income children. Focusing on child welfare economic security, health/mental health, and juvenile justice, NCYL aims to ensure that children receive adequate resources, support, and opportunities so that their future lives will be healthy and productive. NCYL publishes a quarterly legal journal, *Youth Law News*.

National Youth Rights Association (NYRA)

1101 Fifteenth Street, NW, Suite 200
Washington, DC 20005
(202) 835-1739
website: www.youthrights.org

Led by youth, NYRA is a national non-profit organization whose goal is to end age discrimination against young people and ensure their civil rights and liberties. NYRA's ten thousand members, from all fifty states, advocate for lower voting and drinking ages, repeal of curfew laws, and protection of student rights.

For Further Reading

Books

Sarah Elliston, *The Best Interests of the Child in Healthcare*. New York: Routledge-Cavendish, 2007.

Maurene J. Hinds, *You Have the Right to Know Your Rights: What Teens Should Know*. Berkeley Heights, NJ: Enslow, 2005.

David L. Hudson, *The Right to Privacy*. New York: Chelsea House, 2010.

Catriona Macleod, *'Adolescence,' Pregnancy, and Abortion: Constructing a Threat of Degeneration*. New York: Routledge, 2011.

Heather Munro Prescott, *The Morning After: A History of Emergency Contraception in the United States*. New Brunswick, NJ: Rutgers University Press, 2011.

Matthew Waites, *The Age of Consent: Young People, Sexuality, and Citizenship*. New York: Palgrave Macmillan, 2005.

Periodicals and Internet Sources

Priscilla Alderson, Katy Sutcliffe, and Katherine Curtis, "Children's Competence to Consent to Medical Treatment," *Hastings Center Report*, November–December 2006. www.thehastingscenter.org.

Heather Boonstra and Elizabeth Nash, "Minors and the Right to Consent to Health Care," *Guttmacher Report on Public Policy*, August 2000. www.guttmacher.org.

Caitlin Borgmann, "Abortion Parental Notice Laws: Irrational, Unnecessary and Downright Dangerous," *Jurist*, July 27, 2009. jurist.law.pitt.edu. www.jurist.org.

Steve Chapman, "The Perils of a Lower Drinking Age," *Reason* .com, August 21, 2008. http://reason.com.

Erika Christakis, "The Argument You *Don't* Hear About Birth Control in Schools," *Time*, September 26, 2012. www.time .com.

Melinda T. Derish and Kathleen Vanden Heuvel, "Mature Minors Should Have the Right to Refuse Life-Sustaining Medical Treatment," *Journal of Law, Medicine, and Ethics*, Summer 2000.

Frank F. Furstenberg Jr., "On a New Schedule: Transitions to Adulthood and Family Change," *The Future of Children*, Spring 2010.

Kristin Henning, "The Fourth Amendment Rights of Children at Home: When Parental Authority Goes Too Far," *William and Mary Law Review*, October 2011. http://wmlawreview.org.

Human Rights Watch, "My So-Called Emancipation: From Foster Care to Homelessness for California Youth," May 2010. www .hrw.org/sites/default/files/reports/us0410webwcover.pdf.

Tara L. Kuther, "Medical Decision-Making and Minors: Issues of Consent and Assent," *Adolescence*, Summer 2003.

Rich Lowry, "Schools for Contraception," *National Review Online*, September 25, 2012. www.nationalreview.com.

"Not Every Political Policy Has to Be a Calculated Game," *Maclean's*, November 17, 2012. www.macleans.ca/politics /not-every-political-policy-has-to-be-a-calculated-game.

John M. McCardell Jr., "Let Them Drink at 18, with a Learner's Permit," Room for Debate, *New York Times*, May 28, 2012. www.nytimes.com/roomfordebate.

D. Wayne Osgood, E. Michael Foster, and Mark E. Courtney, "Vulnerable Populations and the Transition to Adulthood," *The Future of Children*, Spring 2010.

Sara Rosenbaum, Susan Abramson, and Patricia MacTaggart, "Health Information Law in the Context of Minors," *Pediatrics*, January 1, 2009.

Lainie Friedman Ross, "Health Care Decision Making by Children—Is It in Their Best Interest?" *Hastings Center Report*, November–December 1997.

Joseph J. Sabia and Daniel I. Rees, "The Effect of Parental Involvement Laws on Youth Suicide," *Economic Inquiry*, January 2013.

Index